Thomas A. Williams

A Report Upon the Grasses and Forage Plants and Forage Conditions

of the Eastern Rocky Mountain Region

Thomas A. Williams

A Report Upon the Grasses and Forage Plants and Forage Conditions
of the Eastern Rocky Mountain Region

ISBN/EAN: 9783337317591

Printed in Europe, USA, Canada, Australia, Japan

Cover: Foto ©Andreas Hilbeck / pixelio.de

More available books at **www.hansebooks.com**

BULLETIN No. 12.   Agros. 31.

U. S. DEPARTMENT OF AGRICULTURE.

DIVISION OF AGROSTOLOGY.

[Grass and Forage Plant Investigations.]

A REPORT

UPON THE

GRASSES AND FORAGE PLANTS

AND

FORAGE CONDITIONS

OF THE

EASTERN ROCKY MOUNTAIN REGION.

BY

THOMAS A. WILLIAMS,

ASSISTANT AGROSTOLOGIST.

PREPARED UNDER THE DIRECTION OF THE AGROSTOLOGIST.

WASHINGTON:

GOVERNMENT PRINTING OFFICE.

1898.

LETTER OF TRANSMITTAL.

U. S. DEPARTMENT OF AGRICULTURE,
DIVISION OF AGROSTOLOGY,
Washington, D. C., April 23, 1898.

SIR: I have the honor to transmit herewith, and recommend for publication as Bulletin No. 12 of this Division, a report upon the grasses and forage plants and forage conditions of the eastern Rocky Mountain region, by Thomas A. Williams, assistant agrostologist. Field agents of the division have been carrying on investigations in the region embraced in this report during the past three years, and Mr. Williams, of the division staff, has visited, during the seasons of 1896 and 1897, the more important grazing districts, where, under the direction of the Agrostologist, he has studied the present forage problems of the region and investigated the native grasses and forage plants, noting their characteristics, distribution, general prevalence, and economic importance; he has endeavored to ascertain how the most desirable sorts may be preserved or increased, and has also made close personal observations with the view of determining some practical means of restoring the ranges to their original grazing value, or at least preserving them from further injury through careless and short-sighted practices. The present report is based upon these studies and investigations, as well as upon the results of work done by the field agents of the division. While carrying on these investigations the work of the field agents has not been confined to the districts easily accessible from the railroads and other common lines of travel, but, by means of wagon trips and side excursions on horseback, they have penetrated into the less-known localities, in every case making extensive collections of specimens and seeds, as well as obtaining all the data possible relating to the question of forage supply. One field agent thus covered nearly 1,000 miles in a wagon trip of two months during the past season. (See fig. 1.) There has also been included much valuable information acquired through correspondence with prominent citizens and leading stockmen, who have most cordially responded to letters of inquiry relative to the matters in question and materially aided the Department in the prosecution of these grass and forage-plant investigations. Hearty thanks are here expressed to all those correspondents who have thus cooperated in the work of the division.

3

Some idea of the importance of the subject of this Report upon the Grasses and Forage Plants and Forage Conditions of the Eastern Rocky Mountain Region is indicated by the following statements:

It is estimated from Report No. 7, Division of Statistics, that in the State of Wyoming about 15,000,000 acres are taken up by mountains and forest areas, about 10,000,000 acres are irrigable and hence suitable for general agriculture, while nearly 40,000,000 acres, or almost two-thirds of the entire State, may be regarded as pasture lands only. In Montana the proportion of pasture lands is fully as great as in Wyoming, while in Colorado it will probably fall but little below.

At the beginning of the year 1897 there were in these three States about 350,000 head of horses and mules, valued at about $9,000,000, over 3,000,000 head of cattle, valued at nearly $56,000,000, and over 6,200,000 head of sheep, valued at over $10,500,000, or a total valuation for the stock supported chiefly by these native pasture and meadow lands of about $75,500,000.

The first report on the investigations of the forage plants of the Northwest, from this division, was Bulletin No. 5, on the Grasses and Forage Plants of the Rocky Mountain Region, by P. A. Rydberg and C. L. Shear. This was followed by Bulletin No. 6, on the Grasses and Forage Plants of the Dakotas, by T. A. Williams, aided by Prof. M. A. Brannon, of North Dakota, and E. N. Wilcox and David Griffiths, of South Dakota. Embracing much the same field is Prof. L. H. Pammel's Notes on the Grasses and Forage Plants of Iowa, Nebraska, and Colorado, published as Bulletin No. 9 of this Division; and another, on The Red Desert of Wyoming and its Forage Resources, by Prof. Aven Nelson, is now in press. In the present bulletin the topographical features of the region are considered, including a discussion of the soil, water supply, etc. This is followed by detailed accounts of the cultivated grasses and forage plants and the more important forage plants, both grasses and species of other families, native to the region, concluding with suggestions on methods of improvement of the forage conditions of the ranges.

Respectfully,   F. LAMSON-SCRIBNER,
                                                      Agrostologist.

Hon. JAMES WILSON,
        Secretary of Agriculture.

CONTENTS.

ILLUSTRATIONS.

6

A REPORT UPON THE GRASSES AND FORAGE PLANTS AND FORAGE CONDITIONS OF THE EASTERN ROCKY MOUNTAIN REGION.

INTRODUCTION.

Stock raising will always be an important industry in the vast expanse of territory lying between the Rocky Mountains and the one-hundredth meridian. The early settlers recognized its many natural advantages for this purpose, and at once began to cover the hills and valleys with cattle and other stock. Under the stimulating influence of high prices, resulting largely from the demand created by the civil war, stock raising rapidly grew to be an industry of immense proportions. At first forage was plentiful; everywhere the supply seemed inexhaustible, and the ranchman's chief concern was to get more stock in order that he might turn into cash the grasses of the prairies. Stock grew and fattened on no other feed than the native grasses throughout the entire year.

At length, however, stockmen became aware of the fact that not only was there a possibility, but a probability, that the supply of forage would soon be exhausted if they continued to follow the old methods of stock raising. Under this old system of mismanagement the ranges were stocked to their utmost capacity, even for the most favorable conditions, and consequently the past series of dry seasons resulted in a great shortage of feed. Ranchmen are already confronted with the necessity of providing extra forage supplies for use in seasons when the grasses on the range are short.

With a view to finding some practical means of bettering existing conditions and encouraging stockmen in their efforts to grow forage crops, a series of investigations of the various forage problems existing in the West and Northwest, particularly in the States of Montana, Wyoming, and Colorado, is being carried on by the direction of the Secretary of Agriculture through the Division of Agrostology. These investigations are designed to secure full and accurate information regarding the present condition of the forage problem; what the greatest needs are, and how they can be met in the most practical manner; to study the native grasses and forage plants, their characteristics, distribution, abundance, and value; to ascertain the best means of preserving the more desirable sorts, and to introduce into cultivation such as promise to be of value; to devise some practical treatment for the

7

ranges which will not only restore their original grazing value but guard against future injury through overstocking and other careless and shortsighted practices.

The information upon which this report is based has been gathered from various sources. During the past three seasons field agents of the division have been working in the different parts of the region in question studying matters pertaining to the forage supply. The writer has made two trips into the more important grazing districts, and, under the direction of the chief of the division, has studied the conditions and needs by consulting with the stockmen and collecting all facts likely to aid in the work of getting at a practical solution of the

FIG. 1.—In the field.

various forage problems confronting the people at the present time, and thereby laying the foundations for more intelligent and economical practices in the future.

In April, 1897, the following circular letter with the appended questions was sent to prominent stockmen, farmers, and others interested in the forage problem:

UNITED STATES DEPARTMENT OF AGRICULTURE,
DIVISION OF AGROSTOLOGY,
Washington, D. C., April, 1897.

DEAR SIR: Under the direction of the Secretary of Agriculture this division is investigating the forage question in the Northwest, particularly in the States of Montana, Colorado, and Wyoming. In this investigation particular attention is being given to the native grasses and forage plants, their characteristics, distribution, abundance, and value; the best means of preserving the more valuable kinds, and the methods to be employed in reclaiming those ranges which have been rendered of little or no value for grazing, through overstocking or other causes. In order to obtain a more definite idea as to what the present conditions and greatest needs are, and to gain all possible information that will aid us in determining the most practical methods of improving these conditions, by the introduction and cultivation of new grasses and forage plants or by the preservation and cultivation of native species, correspondence is hereby invited with all interested in the development and preservation of the stock-raising and dairying industries.

There are over 225 different grasses native to this region, and it would be difficult to give an adequate estimate of their immense value as a natural resource. Ever since the Northwest has been settled these grasses have been the chief source of food for the many thousands of horses, cattle, and sheep raised there, and many of them will undoubtedly prove more valuable under cultivation than they are in the native state.

Any assistance you may render in this undertaking, either by sending us the names and addresses of leading farmers, stock raisers, and dairymen of your region, or by furnishing information relative to the points above indicated, will be highly appreciated

Yours, truly,
F. LAMSON-SCRIBNER,
Agrostologist.

Approved:
JAMES WILSON,
Secretary of Agriculture.

(1) What is the chief forage problem in your section—that is, do you need hay plants, soiling crops, drought-resistant crops, winter forage, or early spring or late autumn forage?

(2) How many head of cattle, horses, or sheep can be safely pastured to the square mile under existing conditions?

(3) Has the stock-carrying capacity of the ranges and pastures in your section been diminished through overstocking or other causes? If so, to what extent?

(4) What treatment do you recommend for restoring, renewing, and improving the ranges where they have been overstocked?

(5) What are the most highly valued native grasses and forage plants, and are there any tame grasses or forage plants which might be profitably introduced on the ranges to take the place of the valuable wild grasses of former years?

(6) What is the general character of the land in your locality, and what grasses flourish best on it?

Answers were received from about 600 persons, and the following may be taken as representative of the ideas expressed by the great majority of them.

From Governor Robert B. Smith, of Montana, the following answers were received:

(1) We need drought-resistant crops and winter forage.

(2) Fifty head of horses or cattle or 250 sheep.

(3) Where sheep range, destroyed at least one-half.

(4) If sheep were compelled to be kept in certain portions of the range and the remainder left free for cattle or horses, the range would be fully restored in three years. Sheep destroy the range; cattle and horses do not.

(5) Blue-joint and buffalo-grass are the best native grasses. Do not know of any tame grasses to take their places.

(6) Light gravelly land; soil not deep but rich, and with large per cent of alkali. Buffalo-grass and blue-joint flourish best.

From Hon. John C. Bell, M. C., of Colorado:

(1) In the Uncompahgre, Gunnison, and Grand valleys, the San Luis Valley, and the upper portion of the Arkansas Valley, our great field plant is alfalfa. The mountain sides, mesas, and foothills are covered with bunch grass which supplies all herds from about April 1 to December 1. If we could find some grass that would flourish in the low foothills without irrigation for winter feed it would be a great boon to all of Colorado. Our summer forage is ample and of the very best quality.

(2) The ranges vary so that no approximate estimate can be made. On some high mesas where the snow is deep in winter the grass is very abundant, but lower down it decreases. But these ranges are ample for all the stock that can be wintered in the valleys below.

(3) Not in the mountainous regions.

(4) Cattle and horses rarely impoverish a range, as they do not feed in close bunches, but sheep tramp out and practically destroy the grasses wherever they are kept. Horses and cattle will not remain or feed with them on the range.

(5) Bunch-grass and blue-stem in the mountain regions can not be surpassed unless some grass could be found that would stand the drought in the foothills.

(6) We have three varieties—adobe, black loam soil on the river bottoms, and the high "red oxide" mesa lands. Vegetables grow best on the black loam, wheat and oats on the adobe, fruit trees and alfalfa on the high mesa, though it is all better than the average lands of the country for any of the ordinary crops, and would probably produce most of the common grasses, though but little experiment has been made in this direction.

From Hon. Jos. M. Carey, Cheyenne, Wyo.:

(1) The introduction of a forage plant that will mature during our short seasons and will afford good grazing all the year, the seed of which would germinate and grow by simply being raked or "disked in" on the native sod. The native grasses are so valuable that it would be unwise to destroy them, but with nutritious grasses to supplement them the capacity of a given section for grazing purposes might be greatly increased.

(2) This depends upon circumstances. Some sections as they were left by nature would scarcely carry an animal; others, 30 to 40 head. Should say average 15 head for three hundred and sixty-five days.

(3) Yes; but as soon as cattle are removed the ranges again grow up to the native grasses. When I speak of cattle I mean neat cattle and horses. Where sheep graze for a number of years weeds take the place of native grasses.

(4) Rest.

(5) Bunch-grass, blue-stem, and buffalo-grass are the varieties best known to stockmen. I do not know of any.

(6) Sod free from brush of any kind. The native grasses referred to; with irrigation all of the small grains and forage plants that are common in this latitude produce well. Alfalfa does well everywhere in this State when irrigated, where the altitude is not over 5,000 feet. Three crops may be harvested; season's production, from 3 to 6 tons an acre.

A glance through this correspondence shows at once that not one but many problems relating to the forage supply demand attention. Localities having like soil and climatic conditions may still differ widely as to the most pressing needs. Thus, in one locality the greatest need may be early spring forage, in another it may be winter forage, and in still another it may be summer feed, while in many localities it is a question of a general shortage for the entire year.

The study of the forage question in the West and Northwest has not

been carried far enough to give us solutions to all the problems confronting the stockman; but it has been sufficient to reveal pretty clearly
the causes that have led up to the present exhausted condition of the
range. It shows that the past methods of handling the range have
been shortsighted, and that while these practices are being in a measure corrected by the natural course of events, it is imperative that steps
should be taken to restore and preserve the productiveness of the native
meadow and pasture lands before the destruction has gone too far.
The improvement in the native forage noticeable in some localities during the past one or two seasons is likely to be but temporary, as already
stockmen in these localities are trying to increase their herds, and the
lands will soon be overstocked again.

The investigation has also resulted in a large amount of valuable
data regarding the native grasses and forage plants, the wealth of species found in the region, their value in the natural condition, and their
possibilities under cultivation. There can scarcely be any doubt that
some of these native forms will ultimately become as valuable for
general cultivation as many of the so-called "tame" sorts.

GENERAL TOPOGRAPHICAL FEATURES OF THE REGION.

The topographical features of the three States comprising the greater
part of the Eastern Rocky Mountain region are, in many respects, very
similar. The continental divide, which traverses Montana about 100
miles east of the western boundary and nearly parallel with it, enters
Wyoming a little to the southward of the northwestern corner of that
State and continues its general trend to the southeast until it reaches
central Colorado, where it turns rather abruptly to the southwest.
Approximately five-sixths of Montana, three-fourths of Wyoming, and
two-thirds of Colorado lie east of this divide. While in each State the
greater part of the mountain area is found in the immediate vicinity of
this divide, numerous outlying ranges occur which exert a great influence, not only upon the physical character of the country, but also
upon the climatic conditions, particularly in the distribution of the
moisture; as, for example, the Big and Little Belt Mountains, Snow
Mountains, Bears Paw Mountains in Montana, Shoshone Mountains,
Big Horn Mountains, Bear Lodge Mountains, and Laramie Mountains,
in Wyoming, and the Sangre de Cristo and other ranges in Colorado.

In most cases the mountains along the main divide are rugged, with
precipitous sides, more or less thickly covered with timber, which is
chiefly evergreen, or coniferous. Sometimes the forest covering is so
heavy that the growth of grasses is very limited, but usually there are
numerous "parks" or "opens," in which flourish certain grasses and
other forage plants. The slopes of the mountain ranges are cut up by
numerous gulches and canyons, through which flow streams of water,
fed largely by the melting snows on the mountain tops. The valleys
of these streams widen out here and there into grass-covered areas of

various sizes, forming the "mountain meadows" for which this region is justly famous. The valleys of many of the larger mountain streams, uniting with those of their more important tributaries, often form areas of considerable extent, in which, because of the rich soil and abundant supply of moisture, luxuriant growths of native grasses are produced. These areas, variously called "basins," "parks," etc., protected as they are by mountains on all sides and provided with an abundance of excellent forage and pure water, are magnificent natural pastures, whose only drawback is that often the altitude is so high and the snow-fall is so great that they can be used for only a limited portion of the year. (See fig. 2.) Excellent examples of these areas are Spanish Creek basin, in southern Montana; Centennial Valley, at the head of the Little Laramie River, in Wyoming, and the numerous "parks" of Colorado.

FIG. 2.—The ideal summer range. (From photograph by Prof. A. Nelson.)

In some of the outlying ranges the mountains are less rugged, the slopes are often but sparsely or not at all wooded, and hence offer pro-portionately larger forage producing areas. For example, the Big Horn and Bear Lodge ranges, in Wyoming, contain large areas of grass lands, the former expanding toward the south into a broad, irregular plateau, a very considerable portion of which is covered with a fine sod of native grasses. In many portions of this region the mountains are fringed with an irregular series of foothills, which pass sometimes abruptly, sometimes gradually, into table-lands or mesas, and these in turn are followed by broad valleys and open prairies or plains proper. The frequent arrangement of the land along streams into terraces or successive "benches" is of considerable importance from an agricul-tural point of view, since very often the table-lands differ considerably from the valleys below as to the supply of moisture and the earliness and length of the growing season. This is well illustrated by the Gallatin Valley about Bozeman, Mont., where the season is much earlier on the table-lands. Often it is a difficult matter to get water for irrigation upon these benches, and farmers must depend upon the snow and rain for the supply of moisture for their crops. Along some of the streams, as in the case of the Big Horn River in Wyoming, there are no benches or terraces, the valley being limited by high, abrupt bluffs leading to the uplands which rise gradually to the foothills and mountains.

Extending to the eastward from the principal ranges of the Continental Divide are the vast stretches of level plain, rolling prairie, and rough, eroded bad lands, constituting the great range region east of the Rocky Mountains. Over a considerable portion of this region rugged buttes are scattered here and there in addition to the previously mentioned outlying mountains, relieving the monotony of prairie and plain and affording welcome landmarks for the cowboy and traveler. Occasionally considerable portions of the plains area are cut off from the remainder by natural barriers of hills and mountain ranges, forming drainage basins of considerable extent, as in the case of the Judith basin, in Montana, and the Big Horn basin and the Laramie plains, in Wyoming.

THE SOIL.

The character of the soil in the eastern Rocky Mountain region is exceedingly varied. According to Prof. W. C. Knight, "the various geological formations which have entered into the soils of Wyoming range from Archæan to the Pliocene Tertiary," and the great variability in the composition of the different soils is readily explained from the fact that "some of them have been derived from the entire series of rocks ranging from the Archæan to the close of the Tertiary, while others are the result of the decaying of a single geological horizon." These statements are essentially true of Montana and Colorado. The soil in the valleys varies from light sandy loam to a heavy black loam or a stiff clay. Sometimes a great deal of gravel is present, and often, particularly in the higher valleys, the surface is strewn with bowlders of various sizes brought down by glaciers or mountain torrents. These bowlders are particularly abundant in the valleys of some of the streams rising in the Big Horn, Shoshone, and Medicine Bow mountains, often rendering it practically impossible to drive through with a wagon. The ranchers assert that when the land is brought under irrigation these bowlders gradually work into the soil and in a few years all the smaller ones disappear beneath the surface, making it possible to use the land for hay meadows. The soil is usually fertile and gives excellent yields of grass. In many places the clay contains quantities of "alkali" and constitutes the so-called "gumbo" and "adobe" soils. The soil of the foothills and mesas is usually quite sandy or gravelly, and is warmer, and hence earlier, than the heavier soil of the valleys. On the prairies and plains the soil varies from a sandy to a clay loam, in some places thick and well supplied with humus, in others thin and poor. Throughout the greater part of this region the subsoil is clayey, but in some localities, particularly near the mountains, where the drift and wash is great, it may be quite gravelly in nature. Over the entire region, outside of the mountains and higher foothills, the soil is characterized by the presence of a greater or less amount of alkali. In the well-drained soils of the foothills, mesas, and rolling prairies the amount of alkali present is usually small, but in the broad, flat valleys and level plains it is often large—sometimes so great as to completely change the character of the vegetation. (See fig. 3.) The water from rains and melting snows passes over and through the surface soil and leaches out the alkali, which is carried to the streams, lakes, and ponds. Naturally, much of this water is gathered into low places in the plains and valleys, where it is evaporated rapidly, leaving the alkali in the surrounding soil. In many places the alkali has been brought to the surface in considerable quantities as a result of improper irrigation. This is especially likely to occur if water is used in large quantities and then allowed to

FIG. 3.—An "Alkali spot," showing characteristic greasewood vegetation.

evaporate from the surface. This may be avoided in a large degree by frequent and shallow cultivation after each application of water. Often the water used in irrigating is heavily charged with alkali, which, added to that already present in the soil, ultimately renders the latter unfit for the successful growing of the ordinary farm crops. In popular parlance there are two kinds of "alkali" lands—"black alkali" and "white alkali." The former owes its peculiarities to the presence of salsoda (sodium carbonate) and the latter to the presence of Glauber salt (sodium sulphate) and Epsom salt (magnesium sulphate). The "black alkali" is much more injurious to vegetation than the "white alkali," and fortunately is much less common in this region.

THE WATER SUPPLY.

Over a considerable portion of the region under consideration the annual precipitation, or rainfall, is quite limited. In the great plains area it is not probable that the average would be over 10 or 12 inches per annum—more in the favored localities and less elsewhere. On the mountains and in their immediate vicinity water is usually abundant, and were it not for the many lofty peaks, whose perennial snows supply the streams originating in them, the country would be a desert indeed, and agriculture impossible. As it is, the farmer or stockman is filled with joy when he sees the mountain tops becoming whitened with heavy snows; for they promise him a plentiful supply of water for his crops and his stock during the summer months. Countless streams fed by these snows find their way down to the plain, where they unite to form the larger water-courses—the Missouri, Yellowstone, Platte, and Arkansas rivers. Were it possible to properly husband the water flowing in these streams so that it could be distributed over the land when it is most needed, the forage problem would be a simple one and easily settled in a very large portion of this region for a long time to come.

Under the present condition much of the water runs off during the spring freshets and is lost, while crops and stock often suffer severely for water later in the season. This trouble is sometimes aggravated by the removal of the forest cover in the mountains by fires or by the wholesale cutting of timber. The proper maintenance of this forest cover about the source of the streams furnishing water for irrigation is a matter of vital importance to this whole region, and every possible effort should be put forth to secure it from destruction. A correspondent from Routt County, Colo., writes, "The greatest evil to the range is the destruction of the timber and underbrush at the head of the streams through fires," and many other correspondents have expressed similar views. A good illustration of the injurious effect of the destruction of the forest cover was observed the past season in the Big Horn Mountains, where thousands of acres of spruce and pine timber have been killed by fire, allowing the early and rapid running off of water from the melting snows, and a consequent shortage later in the season in the streams depending upon them for their supply.

Out on the plains, away from the mountains, not only is the precipitation less, but the streams are farther apart, and many of them, because of the excessive evaporation or porous character of the bed, become dry during the summer and autumn months, so that the water supply is insufficient for irrigation, and often it is difficult and sometimes even impossible for the rancher to obtain enough to water his stock. Animals wandering back and forth in search of water trample out and destroy many of the valuable grasses which would otherwise be able to survive the drought. During freshets resulting from melting of the snows in the spring on such a wide expanse of territory, with little if anything to retard the rush of the water into the streams and low places, immense quantities of water are entirely lost. Again, the rain often comes in such sudden and violent storms that but a small proportion of it has time to soak into the soil, the rest rushes into the watercourses, and is speedily carried away. Thus many localities suffer from lack of water, although the annual precipitation, could it be preserved, would, perhaps, be amply sufficient for present needs.

The Belle Fourche River drains a considerable territory in northeastern Wyoming, and during the spring it becomes a raging torrent, carrying off immense quantities of water, while it is often so low during the dry season that no water runs through it in the upper part of its course. The construction of reservoirs to catch and retain the water from the rains and melting snow would undoubtedly go a long way toward the solution of the forage question in many localities on the open ranges. In many places there are natural basins which could be made into reservoirs at a very small expense compared with the great good to the farmers and stockmen which this conservation of water would accomplish.

The excessive trampling of the stock and consequent packing of the soil and the destruction of vegetation in the immediate vicinity of the springs and small streams are no doubt largely responsible for the fact that many of them are now dry for some time during the summer and autumn, though in former years they furnished water throughout the season. Very naturally the stock eats the forage nearest to the watering places first. Soon the vegetation becomes closely cropped, and as the animals visit the watering places daily, the plants are allowed no opportunity to recuperate, and as a result the ground is soon almost or quite destitute of vegetation.

PRESENT ASPECT OF THE FORAGE PROBLEM.

The aspect of the forage question has changed very materially throughout the eastern Rocky Mountain region in the past ten or fifteen years. Formerly comparatively little general agriculture was practiced, except in a few localities near the larger cities and towns. Lack of moisture or of facilities for irrigation made it difficult to secure good crops. Many of the early settlers were engaged in mining, and in the eager search for gold and silver found little time or inclination to engage in agricultural pursuits unless forced to do so by the failure of their mining ventures; others, noticing the great abundance of nutritious forage, bent their energies toward getting together as much stock as possible in order that they might take full advantage of this great natural resource. This course soon resulted in the establishment of numerous large ranches, each controlling a wide stretch of territory, and naturally discouraged the taking up of tillable lands for general agricultural purposes. Hence, farming was largely confined to small inclosed areas on the ranches and to the more protected localities near the larger settlements. Owing to the light rainfall during the summer and autumn the native grasses cured on the ground in such excellent condition that little if any hay or grain was necessary to carry the stock through the winter, and the rancher preferred to buy imported flour and canned fruits and vegetables than to bother about farming.

Upon the advent of the recent series of dry seasons it soon became evident that the ranges were too heavily stocked. Ranchmen were forced to provide forage for their stock in order to carry it through the winter. This has led to the fencing of hay meadows and the cultivation of alfalfa, timothy, and other hay and forage crops. But this made stock raising more expensive and forced many of the large concerns to go out of business. Then, too, as irrigation began to be practiced it soon became evident that many portions of the region were adapted to general farming, and settlers began to take up the land along the streams and to plant it to crops of various kinds. This interfered with the methods of ranging stock practiced on the large ranches, and the stockmen were forced to reduce their herds or seek new ranges. Very often it was found to be more profitable to divide the big ranch into small holdings and sell or rent to farmers and small ranchmen than to continue in the stock business.

In many instances the stockmen owned but little, or none, of the land over which their stock grazed, and their improvements were of little value. In other cases large tracts of land had been purchased or leased and considerable sums of money expended in building fences and making other improvements. As the country has become more and more settled, the former class has largely disappeared. The ranches of the latter class have either accommodated themselves to the changed conditions and developed into the large successfully conducted stock-growing establishments of to-day or have given way entirely to the smaller ranch and farm, where a combination of stock raising and crop growing is practiced.

This changed condition of things is very apparent in northern Wyoming, where in many places the land of the valleys has recently been brought under irrigation and affords fine crops of wheat, oats, rye, barley, early corn, timothy, clover, redtop, and alfalfa. On the Gray Bull River and elsewhere in the Big Horn Basin the change has been brought about largely within the past five or ten years. Instead of the large herds, controlled by a comparatively few wealthy men or by stock companies, the tendency is toward the smaller herds of the individual rancher. Instead of depending so largely upon the Southwest for young cattle the ranchmen are beginning to raise more young stock themselves, and they are beginning to handle better-bred animals and to bring them to a marketable condition at an earlier age.

One of the most pressing needs of this region is a hay plant that will endure the dry weather and afford profitable yields. In localities where water can be had for irrigation there is usually little difficulty in raising plenty of alfalfa, and then the need is for a supplementary hay or forage of some sort in order that the alfalfa may be fed to the best advantage. For much the greater portion of the region, however, irrigation is either impossible or impracticable, and here a drought-resistant grass or forage crop is very much needed. Nearly six hundred farmers and stockmen, representing nearly every county in the States of Colorado, Wyoming, and Montana, and many from adjoining States, in answer to the question, what is your present greatest need in the way of forage, place hay and winter forage first, almost without exception. In some localities winter pasturage is deemed more necessary than hay or coarse forage, but with the changes in the methods of handling cattle and the growing tendency toward winter feeding the use of various kinds of hay and fodder crops is yearly becoming more general. This, together with the fact that in many localities the range has been so reduced by drought and overstocking that it is hardly sufficient for summer paturage alone, making winter feeding absolutely necessary, renders the demand for hay and fodder crops imperative. Then again, the heavy losses of stock during some of the severe storms of recent years have taught the ranchmen the necessity of providing winter feed as a precautionary measure, if for no other reason.

Of scarcely less importance than winter feed, and by some ranchmen regarded of even more importance, is the need of early pasturage. There is a period of a month or more, after the breaking up of winter and before the native grasses get started, which is one of the most critical for the ranchmen of this region. Stock is more or less weakened as a result of the winter season, and palatable food is usually exceedingly scarce. The stockmen say that if some grass could be introduced that would provide pasturage earlier than the native grasses do, it would be worth many thousands of dollars to them annually.

Another matter of great importance to the ranchmen of the Northwest is the question of autumn forage. The native grasses on the open ranges dry up in the latter part of the summer. Formerly the growth was sufficiently abundant to provide plenty of well-cured nutritious forage, but now the ranges are so bare in many localities at the end of the summer that stock can get practically no autumn grazing outside of the fenced areas. Near the mountains the custom is to range the stock in the higher foothills and mountain valleys during the summer, and upon the appearance of the early snows to take it down into the lower foothills, where it is kept during the autumn, or often the entire winter; but in many places drought and overstocking have so depleted these fall and winter grazing lands that they now afford comparatively little forage and are becoming covered with worthless weeds. In such localities it is necessary to begin feeding the stock long before winter begins in order to keep it in good condition. The rancher regards as his most favorable season one in which there is a heavy rainfall during the spring and early summer months, a dry autumn and an open winter, with little snowfall or with high winds to blow the snow into the ravines and gullies. This gives a heavy growth of grass, which cures on the ground, where it can be grazed by the stock during the late fall and winter.

A considerable portion of this region has an altitude too great for the successful growing of alfalfa and other commonly cultivated forage crops, although it includes a great deal of rich land well supplied with natural moisture or capable of being irrigated readily. Thus in Montana the altitudinal limit for the successful growing of alfalfa ranges from about 4,500 to 5,000 feet, and more than one-half of the total area of the State is above this limit; in Wyoming its altitudinal limit seems to be not far from 5,000 feet, and over three fourths of the State is above this altitude; in Colorado it can be successfully grown up to about 6,500 feet in the northern and 7,500 feet in the southern part of the State, and nearly one-half of the State is above this limit. Timothy can usually be successfully grown at an altitude of from 500 to 1,000 feet above that of the limit for alfalfa, and hence replaces it to a greater or less extent, but there is a very decided demand by the farmers and stockmen for a forage crop adapted to these higher altitudes. Mr. T. P. McDonald, of Carbon County, Mont., expresses the sentiment of many when he writes, "We need a good forage plant that will grow and mature above the 5,000-foot level."

In addition to the above-mentioned needs, all of which are of quite general importance, there are many of more or less local significance demanding the attention of the investigator and the farmer. Although alfalfa and other coarse crops can be raised successfully in most localities and are good for hay, they are not satisfactory for general pasturage, and there is a demand for a good pasture grass to be grown under irrigation. In other localities the land is too strongly impregnated with alkali, either from natural causes or through injudicious irrigation, for the successful cultivation of the ordinary forage crops, and plants are desired that will flourish on such soil. In still other localities, particularly near the larger cities and towns, crops suitable for soiling are needed.

In some instances the present lack of forage is due quite as much to the slowness of the farmers and stockmen to adapt themselves to the existing conditions as it is to the want of suitable crops for cultivation. It is hard to get out of the old slip-shod ways, even though it is known that a little well-directed effort will make a given amount of land yield several times as much forage as it did formerly. Careful attention to the development of native meadows and pastures and a more general cultivation of miscellaneous forage crops that can be grown with at least a fair degree of success in nearly all localities will do much toward solving the forage problem.

The effect of such effort is well illustrated by the excellent native meadows that have been produced by intelligent irrigation, examples of which may be seen along the valleys of the Platte, Bear, Gallatin, and Belle Fourche rivers, in the Big Horn Basin, as well as along many other streams of the region. On the other hand, the injurious effect of careless treatment is very apparent on many ranches where, because there is a great abundance of water, the meadows are kept so wet that the better grasses are driven out and their places taken by sedges and rushes, producing an inferior quality of hay.

The following description of the conditions prevailing on the range between the Missouri River, in South Dakota, and the Upper Belle Fourche River, in Wyoming, may be taken as typical of those obtaining over the Northwest generally and illustrative of the marked effect that an isolated mountainous region like the Black Hills may have upon forage production and agriculture in general. The notes were taken during a wagon trip from the Cheyenne Indian Agency, on the Missouri River, up the Moreau River and across to the Belle Fourche River, in northeastern Wyoming, and back through the southern Black Hills to Pierre, S. Dak.

FORAGE CONDITIONS ON THE RANGE OF WESTERN SOUTH DAKOTA AND NORTHEASTERN WYOMING.*

CHEYENNE AGENCY TO BELLE FOURCHE RIVER.

This region varies greatly in the character of its surface. The land near the streams, especially the Moreau and the Missouri rivers, is exceptionally rough. There are no great elevations or depressions, but the smaller ones are a host. Back 3 or 4 miles from the river there are table lands of considerable extent which are comparatively level, even in the lower course. Farther west the country is not so rough, the region from the mouth of Thunder Creek to the Belle Fourche being an undulating prairie.

The soil over a large part of the eastern portion of the region resembles that east of the Missouri River very much. The humus decreases gradually to the westward and one encounters more gumbo. The whole region is covered with grass except occasional small spots of gumbo and the steeper bluffs along the Moreau and Missouri rivers. The eastern portion of the region differs from the western also in having fewer sandy knolls.

All the streams tributary to the Moreau and Cheyenne are wooded to some extent. There are two or three conditions which are suggestive in regard to the growth of timber. The soil is heavy and does not allow the water to percolate through it very easily, but when once started washes badly. This leads to washouts and holes in the stream

*Abstract from the report of Mr. David Griffiths, who served as field agent for the division in South Dakota and Wyoming under a commission extending from the middle of July to the middle of September, 1897.

beds which hold water until late in the summer. The trees getting started around these water-holes are supplied with sufficient moisture during the growing season. The stockmen and Indians have exercised much vigilance of late in keeping out fires. Near Bixby it was stated that it has been ten years since fire has passed over that region.

When fire does get started, it is not so destructive to trees and shrubbery as it would be if there was more grass on the ground. Almost invariably we found the feed very short near the water-holes. During the summer the range cattle feed near the water, working back on to the open range as feed conditions demand. Consequently, by the time vegetation is dry enough to burn, the grass in the vicinity of the water-holes is very short and fire does not do so much damage.

The timber along the Moreau is made up of cottonwood, willows, buffalo berry, box elder, green ash, white elm, plums, and cherries, with buck-bush, poison oak, and various species of rose as undershrubs. On the bluffs on either side are found *Rhus trilobata* and an occasional red cedar. Sage-brush (*Artemisia longifolia*) is common over limited areas in the western portion of the region, while species of cactus are common everywhere.

FIG. 4.—Fresh-water cord-grass (*Spartina cynosuroides*): *a*, spikelet, showing three stamens; *b*, spikelet, showing the projecting stigmas of the pistil; *c*, the same, with the outer glumes removed.

The feed on the Indian reservation is much superior to that farther west, the main reason for this being that it is not pastured so closely. The Indians have only a few cattle, and it appeared that they were taking considerable pains to keep the feed along the Moreau River for winter use. However this may be, we saw but few cattle on the river bottom while on the reservation. Neither were any Indians seen excepting at three points on the river. Their log houses and stables were in evidence all along, but no Indians or cattle to speak of. They were congregated at White Horse camp and the agency. Near each one of these houses was a small piece of ground, from 2 to 3 acres, fenced and under cultivation. Their crops consist of corn, potatoes, pumpkins, and melons. These were usually well tended and a good crop. There were a few pieces of wheat which were an average crop. The Indians evidently do not cultivate the same piece of ground for many years in succession. It was not an uncommon thing to find patches of ground, which had once been under cultivation, all grown up to weeds, and the fence removed from it, possibly to get fresh soil, but probably more often to get rid of the weeds. It was learned that the Indians make almost no preparation for winter feeding, except to save, as much as possible, the feed around their winter quarters. As they have but a small bunch of cattle, they are able to keep close watch of them. Quite a number of cattle were seen which were being driven down to the agency to be sold for beef. They were invariably in good condition.

After leaving the Missouri bottoms no big sand-grass (*Calamovilfa longifolia*) was noticed until the party arrived at the Moreau near White Horse camp. Big cord-grass (*Spartina cynosuroides*) (fig. 4) is the principal grass along the ravines and gullies, and big sand-grass is very common on the knolls farther west. The distribution of big sand-grass, of course, throws much light on the character of the soil. Both of these grasses were pastured closely in the western portion of the region where the feed was short. Usually these grasses are not cut for hay, but this season it is said that they will form the bulk of it, owing to the scarcity of wheat-grass.

Prairie June-grass (*Koeleria cristata*) is a much more important grass on the high prairie in the eastern portion of this region than anywhere else we visited. The small table lands back 3 or 4 miles from the river invariably contain fine growths of this grass, at times almost to the exclusion of the other grasses. There was a large area near Virgin Buttes that stood 10 inches high and so thick that the heads which were then ripe gave a brown appearance to the whole area. It is very common on all the high ground.

Porcupine-grass (*Stipa spartea*) and needle-grass (*Stipa comata*) are found to some extent all along the Moreau bottoms, the latter becoming a very important pasture grass to the westward. Feather bunch-grass (*S. viridula*) is more important on the highland regions eastward. Here it is a very valuable pasture grass and is often found with western wheat-grass (*Agropyron spicatum*) and blue grama (*Bouteloua oligostachya*) in sufficient quantity to make considerable hay.

The more important grasses and forage plants of the region are as follows: Blue grama (*Bouteloua oligostachya*), western wheat-grass (*Agropyron spicatum*), big blue-stem (*Andropogon provincialis*), prairie June-grass (*Koeleria cristata*), big cord-grass (*Spartina cynosuroides*), needle-grass (*Stipa comata*), feather bunch-grass (*S. viridula*), big sand-grass (*Calamovilfa longifolia*), buffalo-grass (*Bulbilis dactyloides*),

Dakota vetch (*Lotus americanus*), wild rye (*Elymus canadensis*), and *Carex filifolia*. The last is of special value early in the season.

Dakota vetch (*Lotus americanus*) is very abundant along the river bottoms. There are often large patches of it which are almost pure. If this proves valuable under cultivation it will be easily propagated, for it produces an abundance of seed. It has, however, the disadvantage of ripening its seed unevenly. Usually the older pods have burst open before the later ones have ripened.

BUTTE POST-OFFICE TO DEVILS TOWER.

The change that takes place as one proceeds along the Owl Butte road from Dead Horse Creek toward the foothills of the Black Hills is something wonderful. One passes from a region where the ranches are 5 to 40 miles apart, where there is practically no cultivation, and where there is nothing to break the monotony of the scene but bunches of cattle feeding in the "draws" and an occasional patch of scrubby box elder and ash on the creek bottoms, to a thickly settled region, where there are good buildings, excellent crops of grain and hay, and where everything in the shape of vegetation makes a thrifty growth. The greater part of the land along the Belle Fourche from Butte to the Tower is fenced, either for growing cultivated crops or for winter feed. For about half the distance from Butte to Belle Fourche the route was through a narrow lane left for a road and in which there was no feed whatever—everything being pastured closely. The farmers fence their crops, pastures, and hay land, and turn their cattle out into the roads which lead into the Black Hills on one side and into the open range on the other. The party, at times, experienced some trouble in finding feed for their horses.

Nearly everything depends on irrigation here, the water being carried from tributaries of the Belle Fourche by a system of ditches and sluices onto the land. Nowhere is water taken from the Belle Fourche itself, the reason being that the river has not sufficient fall to enable farmers to get the water onto the land without too great an expense. It was learned also that the volume of water in the river fluctuates greatly, a rise of many feet occurring in a few hours at times when heavy rains fall in portions of its drainage basin. Damming has been tried in several localities without success. As the tributaries from the hills are quite numerous, the farmers are usually able, by judicious management, to get a sufficient volume of water for their crops from them. Usually the water is exhausted before the middle of July, but by an intelligent use of their supply during May and June they are able to raise fine crops. In many instances the farmers get along by building a dam across a gully and holding the water derived from melting snows and spring rains until it is needed later in the season. In the immediate vicinity of Belle Fourche opportunity was afforded to study the effect of an abundant supply of water the entire season. It is here obtained from one of the tributaries of the Red Water.

Here was found a most luxuriant growth of both native and cultivated vegetation. As fine fields of wheat were found here as in the great small-grain belt in the eastern part of the State, while the hay crop was something wonderful. The unirrigated lands, however, presented an appearance not unlike the drier portions of the open range farther east.

The principal hay crop is alfalfa, of which, they obtain about 4 tons per acre from three cuttings, which is the usual method of handling. The farmers were experimenting with a fourth cutting this year, and were considerably encouraged over the prospect at the time the region was visited. This crop is prized very highly because of the fact that they are able to get such a yield per acre. Many other hay crops are grown very successfully, but none yields such a quantity of feed as this one.

Redtop makes the finest growth here of any place visited on the trip. On the Seth Bullock ranch there is a large meadow which was sown to redtop and timothy eight or ten years ago. The timothy is now nearly all run out, while the redtop this year is a fine stand about two feet high.

Besides the above may be mentioned timothy, white sweet clover (*Melilotus alba*), millet, and June clover, all of which make good growths. White sweet clover (*Melilotus alba*) is so persistent in its habits that it assumes much of the characteristics of a weed along the ditches and among other perennial forage crops. It makes an immense growth wherever it gets started on irrigated land. At Belle Fourche was seen near a spring about an acre that stood about 9 feet high.

Native grasses are also irrigated with good success. When, however, a piece of ground is irrigated year after year, that invaluable species, *Agropyron spicatum*, runs the other grasses out. Several instances of this were seen and attention was called to it, not only in the vicinity of Belle Fourche, but farther west, in Wyoming, as well. The most striking example was near Snoma, S. Dak., where there was a meadow of 30 or 40 acres of this grass, with a crop of about 2 tons to the acre. About one-fourth of it was headed out. It was raining at the time of the visit and the grass, therefore, looked fresh and thrifty. Such a large field of this glaucous-leafed grass made a very pretty sight. It was ascertained that this meadow had been irrigated and cut for five consecutive years with a good crop of hay upon it each year. Such a condition is really extraordinary, for ranchmen on the range and even the farmers in the eastern part of the State are seldom able to cut crops of this on the same ground for more than two years in succession. Even when pastured closely year after year the quantity of feed becomes very small. But this is simply one more evidence of what a proper amount of water will accomplish when applied to this soil.

Barnyard-grass (*Panicum crus-galli*) makes a fine growth along the ditches and roadsides where the sod has been partially subdued. It has two distinct forms of growth. Along the ditches and among other grasses it assumes an upright form, while along roads and in barnyards, where the ground is packed down to some extent, it is almost prostrate and often strikes root at the joints. It appears to thrive as well under this form of irrigation as it does under artesian irrigation in the eastern part of the State.

Squirrel-tail grass (*Hordeum jubatum*) is a bad weed wherever the perennial grasses are irrigated on low, alkaline ground.

Besides the usual forage crops there is a great deal of rye, wheat, and oats cut for hay. Winter rye is usually sown. These crops are resorted to only in the drier portions of the region or where no water is available for irrigating purposes. Although small grain is raised here successfully with irrigation, the main crop is hay. There is considerable feeding done during the winter. The big cattle companies make provision with the settlers here, and also with the ranchmen farther out on the range, for the wintering of calves and weak cows which are picked up during the last beef "round-up" in the fall.

The distribution of precipitation is very peculiar. The rainfall is much more abundant in the vicinity of the Black Hills than on the open range on either side. While irrigation is resorted to with profit wherever practicable, the region is not dependent on it entirely. Occasionally good crops of grain are raised without irrigation, but it is rather uncertain. When wheat and oats are sown for the grain and the crop proves to be a failure, it can usually be told in time so that it can be cut early enough to make good hay, which is always in demand. In the vicinity of Sundance, Wyo., and elsewhere along the base of the Bear Lodge Mountains, very fair crops are usually raised with no artificial watering. This year the prospects near Sundance were very good, but they had the misfortune of being "hailed" out.

The Bear Lodge Mountains are in general covered with pine (*Pinus scopulorum*), with an occasional grove of oak, poplar, and birch. The pine is especially heavy on the outer slopes of the mountains and in the "draws" and gulches farther up. Along the divides and edges of "draws" there is very fine pasturage. The range cattle do not get in here to any extent, partly from choice but principally on account of the fact that ranchers have fenced most of the land along the base of the mountains separating the open range from the mountain pasture lands. Common along the Bear Lodge Mountains is King's fescue (*Festuca kingii*), which makes a fine growth below the lower timber line and is very common at higher elevations. It is highly prized by the ranchmen along the base of the mountains on account of its early spring growth. It furnishes pasturage at a much earlier date than any other native grass. Occasionally it makes some hay, but it is looked upon as a pasture rather than a hay grass.

As one proceeds up the Belle Fourche from the Tower he can not help but notice the gradual decrease of the pine timber. It becomes more and more scrubby until it practically disappears at the mouth of Wind Creek. On the bluffs on either side of the stream is a growth of pine, with some oak, and on the bottoms there is a good growth of cottonwood, with more or less of the buffalo berry, green ash, box elder, and an occasional plum and cherry thicket. There is always a very vigorous growth of roses, buck-bush, and sage-brush. There are large areas on the bottoms covered with long-leafed sage (*Artemisia longifolia*), almost to the exclusion of other vegetation.

Some difficulty was experienced in finding feed for the horses in the upper Belle Fourche region, not that the country is not productive, but there are too many cattle. It would be difficult to tell what grasses grow on the river bottom were it not for the winter pastures which are fenced in. During the two nights spent here the party managed to camp in these winter pastures where there were good growths of blue grama (*Bouteloua oligostachya*), needle-grass (*Stipa comata*), feather bunch-grass (*S. viridula*), western wheat-grass (*Agropyron spicatum*), prairie June-grass (*Koeleria cristata*), big sand-grass (*Calamovilfa longifolia*), big cord-grass (*Spartina cynosuroides*), slender cord-grass (*S. gracilis*), wild rye (*Elymus canadensis*), sand rush-grass (*Sporobolus cryptandrus*), and Montana sand grass (*Calamagrostis montanensis*). The main hay grass is western wheat-grass, which is cut in fenced areas along the river bottoms and farther back on the range, along creek bottoms. Water for irrigating purposes is rather scarce, but wherever found and used good crops of alfalfa are raised. The rainfall is much less than it is in the vicinity of the Bear Lodge Mountains. As near as we were able to learn the rainfall is seldom sufficient to mature a crop of small grain after one gets 10 miles west of the Bear Lodge Mountains.

It appears to be the common experience that native sod when irrigated grows up almost exclusively to *Agropyron spicatum*, which is known by the name of wheat-grass. Several instances of this were seen—one at Mr. Baugh's, another at Mr. McKean's, farther up the river.

A great deal of the country about Moorcroft is covered with species of sage-brush, salt-sage, greasewood, and cactus. This is in the edge of the sage-brush plains of Wyoming. To the east are the hills, covered with a good growth of pine. This condition continues nearly to Merino, where the railroad works back toward the western timber line of the foothills. The soil is largely of a clayey nature, much of it of the sort popularly called "gumbo," and washes very badly. The rain does not soak into the ground much, but runs off into the streams, often swelling them to enormous extent. Among the sage-brush and cacti are good growths of grasses, generally those which do not form a sod under ordinary conditions. Among the most important may be mentioned needle-grass (*Stipa comata*) and western wheat-grass (*Agropyron spicatum*). On the divides are found big sand-grass (*Calamovilfa longifolia*) and blue grama (*Bouteloua oligostachya*), while big cord grass (*Spartina cynosuroides*) and salt-grass (*Distichlis spicata*) are the most common on the low ground. Needle-grass (*Stipa comata*) is a very important grass in this region. Northwest of New Castle, near the junction of the Burlington and Missouri River Railroad and Skull Creek, it is especially common. In this vicinity and extending southward into the oil regions are large areas among the sage-brush where no other grasses grow.

As one approaches Inyan Kara Mountain the country assumes much the appearance of that around Sundance, as would be expected. There are more streams, and consequently more water available for irrigation. The rainfall is also more abundant, and the soil has more sand and humus in its make-up. The mountain and all the elevations in the neighborhood are covered with pine, while groves of poplar, birch, and oak are common. The creeks have a growth of cottonwood, box elder, and green ash. Springs of pure soft water are common near the base of the mountain.

Near Inyan Kara we found a ranchman drilling with the expectation of getting a flow of water. He started in last year, when he struck a stratum from which water raised within a few feet of the surface. He renewed his efforts this year, hoping to get a sufficient flow to irrigate from. The open range is closely pastured here also. Here again it was learned that until about four years ago hay could be cut anywhere on the upland, but for the past few years the cattle have become so numerous that they keep the grass eaten off so closely that the effect is much the same as successive cutting year after year. Occasionally a ranchman attributes the short crop of the past few years to drought, but the majority of them agree that it is due to overstocking.

We found more and better farming along Skull Creek than along the Upper Belle Fourche. This is probably due largely to the better facilities for irrigation. There are ranches at short distances along the creek, and considerable hay was being put up. Alfalfa is their main crop whenever they can get water onto the land. Timothy is raised to some extent, and rye and oats are common hay crops. No running water was found until the party got down near the Burlington and Missouri River Railroad. There is as good an illustration of the effect of water on the growth of vegetation here as one could wish to see. On the one hand there is a perfect wilderness of sage-brush (*Artemisia longifolia* and *A. tridentata*) as far as the eye can reach, with the usual light growth of grass, forming no sod to speak of; on the other, native grasses, alfalfa, oats, and garden truck make a fine growth with artificial watering.

The arable land in the region between New Castle, Wyo., and Rapid City, S. Dak., is confined to the valleys and creek bottoms which lie between the different ridges in the Black Hills upheaval. The crops raised are about the same as at Belle Fourche and along the eastern foothills. It appears to be the practice in localities here as at Belle Fourche to seed for a crop of grain, and if the yield does not promise well it is cut for hay before it becomes thoroughly ripened. Some very fine crops of alfalfa, wheat, and oats were seen in Spring Creek Valley. Redtop and timothy are common on the larger areas of low ground. Redtop is especially abundant, and there was a fine crop of hay in Rapid Creek Valley to the southwest of Rapid City.

The climatic conditions are in marked contrast with those at a lower elevation. Harvesting was in progress in the vicinity of Belle Fourche the 1st of August, but 20 or 25 days later, when the party crossed the Black Hills on their return trip, a great deal of wheat and oats were still green. Only about one-half of the crop through the hills had been cut at this late date.

A beautiful arrangement of native grasses is found along the foothills near Rapid City. There are a great many cattle pastured here, and the grasses are consequently kept eaten down quite closely. There are

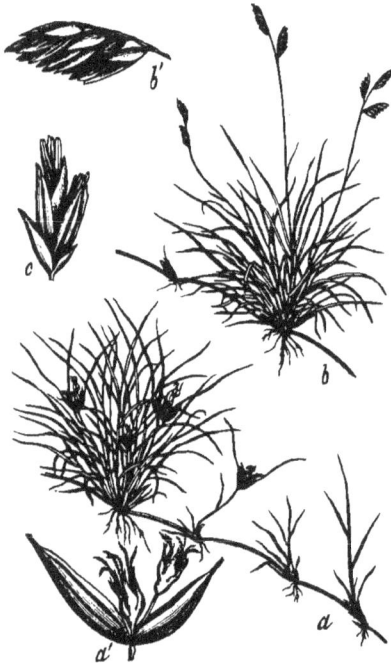

FIG. 5.—Buffalo-grass (*Bulbilis dactyloides*): *a*, female plant; *b*, male plant; *a'*, two clusters of female spikelets; *b'*, a branch of several staminate spikelets; *c*, a male or staminate spikelet of two flowers.

three species, which form a perfect sod in places. The country is rolling—sometimes hilly. In the depressions are patches of ground several acres in extent which are as smooth as though they had been laid out by artificial means. On these areas are full sods of blue grama (*Bouteloua oligostachya*), black grama (*B. hirsuta*), and buffalo-grass (*Bulbilis dactyloides*) (see fig. 5), arranged in natural lawns, as it were, according to nature's own fantastic designs. It made a very pretty sight. No artificial lawn could be more desirable. The color of the grasses, so similar and yet so delicately different that each species growing in separate patches could be recognized at a considerable distance, the splendid sod, and the pleasing general effect suggested the possible use that might be made of these grasses for lawns, borders, and designs about dwellings, public buildings, and cemeteries.

RAPID CITY TO PIERRE.

Nowhere on the trip was better feed found than along the trail from Rapid City to Pierre. No pasturing had been done here except at certain points, as Pœno Hills and Grindstone Buttes. This is due mainly to the fact that our route lay along the divide, where water is scarce. It was the intention of the party to take the Bad River road, and they would have done so had they not been informed that everything was pastured closely all the way. Blue grama (*Bouteloua oligostachya*) makes a fine growth here and was nice and green the 1st of September. Considerable hay was being put up in the eastern portion of the region. It consisted principally of Western wheat-grass (*Agropyron spicatum*) and blue grama (*Bouteloua oligostachya*), together with some feather bunchgrass (*Stipa viridula*) and needle-grass (*S. comata*). In the "draws" there is more of the *Agropyron* and less of the *Bouteloua*. In the larger draws there is a good growth of big cord-grass (*Spartina cynosuroides*) and on the knolls a light growth of big sand-grass (*Calamovilfa longifolia*).

At Pierre the cattlemen were much exercised over the fact that the grass on the range was so backward in ripening. They were fearful lest it should remain green until frost struck it, thereby leaving their winter feed in poor condition. They were therefore well pleased with the hot, dry weather which prevailed during the first ten days in September.

CULTIVATED GRASSES AND FORAGE PLANTS.

The failure of the ranges to supply sufficient forage for all seasons of the year has led to an increased effort on the part of the stockmen and farmers to cultivate the various standard grass and forage crops. In many instances experiments have been made with the different novelties introduced and sold by seedsmen or distributed gratuitously by the United States Department of Agriculture. As was to be expected, the old and so-called "tame" grasses have refused to accommodate themselves to the extreme conditions of soil and climate prevailing in some parts of the region, and while a few of the newly introduced plants have proved valuable, many others have shown themselves to be practically worthless. The "tame" grasses most commonly found in meadows and pastures are timothy, redtop, Kentucky blue grass, smooth or Hungarian brome-grass, meadow fescue, and orchard grass. The millets and the various small grains are quite generally grown for summer forage and for hay, and corn and the sorghums, both saccharine and non-saccharine varieties, are occasionally grown for fodder. Nearly all the common clovers are successfully grown in some part of the region, alfalfa and red clover being in most general cultivation. Very few of the large ranches are without fields of timothy, redtop, clover, or alfalfa; often all are grown on the same ranch. Sometimes these fields cover hundreds of acres and yield thousands of tons of hay. Almost without exception they are irrigated, at least for a portion of the season. In many localities the proprietors of the large ranches prefer not to bother with the extensive cultivation of forage crops that would be necessary to properly feed their herds during the winter, depending upon the small ranchmen and farmers in the valleys for their winter forage supply. The hay is sold to the ranchmen, or more often the cattle are brought to the farmer and he winters them at so much per head. This winter feeding of range stock is becoming quite an industry and could, no doubt, be more generally practiced with advantage to both the large and the small ranch owner. Up to the present time winter feeding is largely, in fact almost entirely, confined to cows, calves, and bulls; the most of the stock being expected to "rustle" its living on the range except during very stormy weather, when a little hay may be fed.

TIMOTHY.

Phleum pratense.

This is more widely cultivated than any other "tame" grass in the eastern Rocky Mountain region. The cheapness of the seed, the ease with which a meadow can be seeded down, and the excellent quality of the hay make this grass a great favorite. In most localities irrigation is necessary to grow it successfully, but with plenty of water enormous yields are often obtained, particularly in the rich valleys in the northern part of the region. Reports of the successful cultivation of this grass have been received from every county in both Montana and Wyoming, and from nearly every county in Colorado, but always under irrigation except in some of the moister valleys in or near the mountains. Sage-brush lands when cleared, irrigated, and seeded to timothy make fine meadows, but the greasewood lands are too strongly impregnated with alkali. Timothy can be grown successfully at a higher altitude than most of the other commonly grown grasses, and is becoming quite generally established in waste places and along trails throughout the entire region. Several of the field agents of the division have reported finding it well established in many places in the mountains. Professor Pammel found it flourishing at an elevation of 10,500 feet in northern Colorado, and the writer found it at a similar elevation in the central part of the State. In the Bear Lodge Mountains and in the Black Hills it is very abundant at 5,000 and 6,000 feet, making a very fine growth, and is spreading very rapidly in moist, open situations along the trails. In the Big Horn Mountains of Wyoming and in the Spanish Basin in Montana it was found to be abundant, growing with alpine timothy (*Phleum alpinum* L.) at from

7,000 to 8,000 feet or more. This ability of timothy to establish itself and thrive at comparatively high altitudes makes it of special value for a large portion of this region. Speaking in this connection Mr. W. S. Coburn, of Delta County, Colo., says "timothy grows to perfection up to an elevation of 9,000 feet," and Mr. T. P. McDonald, of Carbon County, Mont., says "alfalfa and clover do well below the 4,500-foot level, but above that altitude timothy is the most successful."

REDTOP.
Agrostis alba.

This grass stands very close to timothy in its importance as a meadow grass for this region. Its cultivation is less general than that of timothy, however, being more strictly confined to the lower mountain valleys and better irrigated localities, and it is much more generally grown in Montana than in either Wyoming or Colorado. Like timothy, it is becoming well established in the native meadows and waste places. It thrives best on quite moist bottom lands, and is especially valuable on meadow lands liable to overflow. It is a common practice to sow this grass in irrigated native meadows to supplement the native species. It occupies the low marshy places and resists the encroachments of sedges and rushes better than timothy or the common native grasses. Though usually grown in connection with other grasses or with clovers, it makes a fine meadow when grown alone under proper irrigation. One of the finest redtop meadows ever seen by the writer was on a large horse ranch on the Gray Bull River, Wyoming. About 80 acres of the grass were standing at the time of the visit (August, 1897), and some had already been harvested. The land was the common sage-brush land of the valley, and had been given but little cultivation before being seeded down, but was well irrigated. The field was "as even as a floor," and as the mower passed along, it was noticed that the grass came well up along the sides of the horses. Almost all the cultivated land on this ranch was devoted to this crop, which is fed to fine-bred horses.

KENTUCKY BLUE GRASS.
Poa pratensis.

The principal use of Kentucky blue grass in this region is for lawns. With irrigation fine lawns can be made almost anywhere, if the land is not too strongly impregnated with alkali. The great difficulty often experienced in getting a good stand of this grass is one of the chief drawbacks to its culture here. The seed as sold in the markets is too often so poor that the farmer fails to get a good stand for his first sowing and gives up in disgust. Then, again, it takes some time for the grass to form a good sod, and the average Western farmer is too impatient for immediate results to wait for it. Nevertheless this grass is becoming quite abundant in many of the older settled localities and is gradually working its way into the meadows and pastures. Together with Canadian blue grass (*Poa compressa*), low spear-grass (*Poa annua*), and redtop, it follows along the irrigating ditches, forming bright green borders, and affording many juicy mouthfuls for the cattle and other stock. Like most of the other cultivated grasses, it thrives best in the rich valleys of the lower mountains and foothills, where it is protected from drought and the excessive heat of midsummer. It is indigenous in many parts of the Rocky Mountain region.

SMOOTH OR HUNGARIAN BROME-GRASS.
Bromus inermis.

Of all recent introductions smooth brome (see fig. 6) is the most promising hay and pasture grass for the dry portions of the Northwest. Not only does it possess excellent drought-resistant qualities, but it starts much earlier in the season than the common grasses and continues growing well into the autumn, two things very much to be desired in a grass for cultivation in this region at the present time.

In Colorado the grass has been tried in a number of localities with good success. In speaking of grasses for dry situations on the ranges, Mr. R. E. Beatty, of Arapahoe County, says, "*Bromus inermis* comes the nearest to a suitable grass that we have tried so far;" Mr. Thomas R. Pace, of Garnett, "recommends smooth brome-grass," and Mr. George C. Baker, of Mosca, says, "*Bromus inermis* is our best tame grass." It is regarded as the most promising of the introduced grasses tried at the Colorado experiment station.

FIG. 6.—Smooth or Hungarian brome-grass (*Bromus inermis*): *a*, spikelet; *b*, flowering glume seen from the back; *c*, floret seen from the anterior side, showing palea.

The grass seems to have been given less attention in Wyoming than in either Colorado or Montana. Mr. Griffiths, in his report for the past season, speaks of seeing a plot of it on the ranch of Mr. John Baugh, of Carlisle, Wyo. He says,

"Mr. Baugh has been experimenting two years, both with and without irrigation. He seems to think that the smooth brome-grass does not thrive so well under irrigation. The effect of irrigation was really quite peculiar. The irrigated portion of the plot was fresh and green (middle of August) while the unirrigated portion, though it had made a much better growth, was completely dried up. I am not certain but that a thorough wetting at less frequent intervals would have produced better results. He irrigates by means of a tank and windmill. The water is conducted to the garden by a pipe and the crop is sprayed. All his garden truck looked well. Cabbage and tomatoes were especially fine." In Colorado smooth brome has done well under irrigation, particularly when pastured.

In Montana smooth brome has received considerable attention, and reports regarding it are very satisfactory indeed. Hon. Paris Gibson, of Great Falls, says, "In the experiments I have made with new forage plants I find *Bromus inermis* the most hardy. It appears in the spring much earlier than our native grasses." Similar reports were received from Messrs. M. W. Jones and E. Vine, of Miles City, and from Director Emery of the State Experiment Station. Judging from these reports and from the excellent results already obtained in growing this grass in Canada, as well as in the Dakotas and other Northwestern States, it seems probable that smooth brome will prove of great value for cultivation on the dry lands of the Northwest. It should be given a thorough trial, especially as a grass for reseeding worn meadows and pastures.

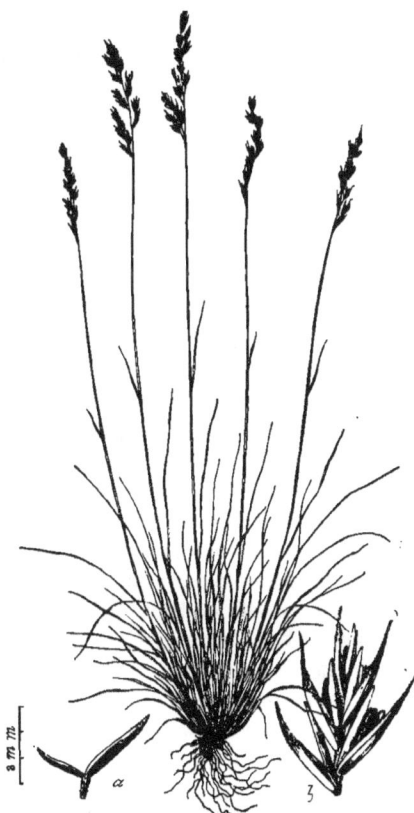

FIG. 7.—Sheep fescue (*Festuca ovina*).

THE FESCUES.

About the only fescue that seems to have been tried to any extent is meadow fescue (*Festuca elatior pratensis*), and this is only occasionally seen in cultivation—usually in mixture with other grasses or with clovers. On rich loamy soils, with abundant irrigation, it seems to do quite well. Favorable reports have been received from several points in central Colorado and central and southern Montana. Mr. Griffiths found it doing well in northeastern Wyoming. It is frequently met with along irrigating ditches and in public parks in the cities and towns, often occurring in waste places as an escape and already well established in favorable situations. It does not seem to thrive in soils containing much alkali. At the Utah Station this grass has been grown with fine success as an element in permanent pastures and meadows, and it is altogether likely that it can be so used in many portions of the Rocky Mountain region. Many native forms of both sheep fescue (*Festuca ovina*) (fig. 7) and red fescue (*Festuca rubra*) occur in this region, and although the cultivated varieties have been given little, if any, attention, it is not unlikely that they could be used to advantage in reseeding the ranges, particularly in the foothills and lower mountains.

ORCHARD GRASS.

Dactylis glomerata.

Like meadow fescue, this grass has received but little attention from farmers and ranchmen in this region. It has been tried at the experiment stations, sometimes with success and sometimes without. It requires fairly rich soil and a reasonable amount of moisture, and hence thrives best on irrigated lands of the valleys and benches. It has succeeded quite well at the Utah station, and good reports of it have been received from central and southern Montana and from many parts of Colorado. It was seen on several ranches near Evanston, Wyo., the past season and was making a fine growth. Mr. W. C. Burke, of Las Animas, Colo., in an answer to the question as to what grasses and forage plants do best in his locality, includes this grass, with the statement that "when irrigated it produces about 2 tons of hay per acre." It is deserving of more general cultivation as an element in mixtures for permanent meadows and pastures and for seeding down sparsely wooded areas.

ALFALFA.

By far the most important forage plant cultivated in this region at the present time is alfalfa. Scarcely a farm or ranch under irrigation can be found in the entire region without its alfalfa field, and on many of the larger ranches hundreds of acres are devoted almost exclusively to this crop. It flourishes on the better drained valley lands and irrigated bench lands in all parts of the region where the altitude is not too great, and alfalfa hay constitutes the principal winter feed for many thousand head of horses, sheep, and cattle. Of recent years it is being extensively used in fattening sheep and cattle for market. There is great need of a good supplementary forage to be fed along with the alfalfa. It is so rich in muscle-making food elements that, as ordinarily fed, its full value is not obtained, and ranchmen are beginning to realize the necessity of mixing it with corn fodder, sorghum, prairie hay, or other forage containing an excess of fat-forming elements in order to feed in the most economical manner.

Three or more cuttings are obtained each season unless, as is often the case, it is more desirable to pasture off the later growth. This is done when summer pasturage is scarce or when there is no market for the hay and the ranchman gets enough for his own use from the first one or two cuttings. During the past season it was learned from several ranchmen in the Big Horn Basin that they very seldom made more than two cuttings, for the reason that they needed no more for wintering their own stock and the price of the hay was so low that it paid them better to pasture their fields for a portion of the season. This was in a region where the summer pasturage was short because of drought and previous overstocking, though at the present time the number of stock kept on the range is undoubtedly much below what the land ought to support under a proper system of grazing and supplementary feeding.

One of the things which makes alfalfa so valuable for this region is its ability to thrive on land containing a considerable quantity of alkali. There are few cultivated crops that will stand as much alkali as this.

The injurious effects of too much water upon the growth of alfalfa is well illustrated by the conditions at present prevailing in a number of localities in Colorado, particularly in the southern part of the State. The soil, either from natural causes or as a result of the methods of irrigation practiced, has become saturated with water to within a short distance of the surface. As a consequence the roots of the alfalfa rot and the plants become sickly and finally die, rendering it impossible to produce anything like a permanent meadow. Here in Colorado, as well as in many other parts of this region, the best success is obtained with alfalfa on the bench lands. It is surprising what a small amount of labor is required to obtain a good alfalfa meadow in some portions of this region. For example, it is a common practice to give sage-brush land no more plowing or other preparation than is necessary in taking off the sage-brush. The brush is cut and grubbed out, raked up and burned, and the seed sown directly on the unplowed land, covered and watered. The soil is so loose as to require little or no stirring, and water is the only thing necessary to make it produce abundant crops of alfalfa. Of course more thorough preparation will give an evener and more lasting meadow, but the writer has seen many fine alfalfa meadows on land untouched by the plow except to make ditches for distributing the water.

RED CLOVER.

Next to alfalfa, red clover is the most widely cultivated leguminous forage crop in this region. It seems to be more generally grown in

Montana than in either Colorado or Wyoming, and its cultivation is chiefly confined to rich valleys and bench lands near the mountains where there is a good supply of moisture or where irrigation is practiced. It is usually grown with timothy and other meadow grasses, and is cut for hay or used as a soiling crop. Very fine crops are raised in central and southwestern Montana and in northern and central Colorado, and it is occasionally seen elsewhere in these States. Red clover is not generally grown in Wyoming, though it is being tried in many localities with very fair success. During the past season it was observed in successful cultivation in Crook, Johnson, Bighorn, and Uinta counties.

ALSIKE.

Although less commonly grown than red clover, alsike is certainly a valuable crop for many parts of this region. Many farmers who have grown them side by side prefer the alsike to the red clover as a forage crop for their respective localities. For example, Mr. C. C. Willis, of Horse Plains, Mont., writes that he much prefers alsike on account of its heavier yield of forage and greater drought-enduring qualities. Excellent fields of alsike and timothy were seen in 1896 in the Gallatin Valley, and reports of the successful growing of this clover have been received from various points in central and southwestern Montana, northern Wyoming, and northern and central Colorado. As a general thing the alsike seems to be hardier than red clover and is better adapted for permanent meadows, and some maintain that it does better on the heavy " gumbo " soil found in so many places in the Northwest. It has also given good results in many parts of the Dakotas, where it has received a thorough trial. It deserves more attention from farmers and ranchmen in the Northwest generally.

WHITE CLOVER.

It is rarely that this clover is sown in this region except on lawns or in dooryards, but its ability to gain a foothold and maintain itself among other vegetation is well shown in the fact that it is found everywhere in patches of various sizes along the margins of irrigating ditches, in waste places, and in pastures and meadows. Reports from several counties in central and western Montana and central Colorado indicate that it is occasionally sown in pastures and is growing in favor, more particularly for use in pastures for sheep and dairy stock. In extended trips through this region in both 1896 and 1897 the writer found but very few instances of its having been sown purposely in pastures, though it was often present even in native pastures in greater or less quantities.

The excellent showing made by this clover during the season of 1897 was very noticeable throughout the West and Northwest generally, particularly in the older-settled districts. In eastern South Dakota, northwestern Iowa, and eastern Nebraska this clover made a remarkable development. Almost everywhere along roadsides, in waste places, and in pastures could be seen the masses of white blossoms. Pastures in which scarcely an appreciable amount of the clover had ever been observed before were white with it. In many cases no clover seed has ever been sown in the pastures, but it has gradually worked in from accidental sources, and though the progress has undoubtedly been slow, it has nevertheless been sure, and this clover has come to occupy a very important place among the vegetation of the pastures. The tendency of white clover to develop in alternating periods of light and heavy growth has often been observed in the past, and its appearance in such quantity in the present instance is a good illustration of the changes in the composition of pastures that are going on constantly, though they are not always for the betterment of the pasture, as in this case.

MISCELLANEOUS FORAGE CROPS.

Aside from the preceding list of standard grasses and forage plants, there are a number of crops of greater or less importance that are grown in the various parts of the region. In most cases their cultivation is not general, sometimes because the plants are not well enough known and sometimes because of their inability to thrive under the conditions prevailing over a large part of the region.

In the dry portions of Colorado where irrigation is not practiced the sorghums, both saccharine and nonsaccharine varieties, are grown to some extent for winter forage and for soiling. The great drought-enduring qualities of the sorghums and their ability to thrive on land containing considerable alkali render them especially valuable for certain portions of this region. Mr. E. E. T. Hazen, of Phillips County, Colo., reports good success in growing several of the nonsaccharine varieties (yellow milo maize, brown doura, and Jerusalem corn), and S. Needham, of Prowers County, regards "sorghum as very valuable for winter forage on nonirrigable lands." Only the early maturing varieties like Early Amber are grown in Wyoming and Montana, and these not to any great extent.

The common cereal crops, such as rye, oats, wheat, and barley, are often grown for forage. Rye and oats are used for this purpose more often than any others, although it is a common practice to cut any cereal for hay if conditions are such that it is not likely to mature a crop of grain. Rye is being very successfully grown for late and early pasturage in many localities, and its cultivation is becoming more general each year. It is already quite extensively grown in central Colorado, northern Wyoming, and some parts of Montana. Sown in early autumn, it gets the benefit of the rains and snows of fall, winter, and early spring, and usually matures a fair crop of grain in addition to furnishing much pasturage, when spring-sown crops would fail unless artificially watered.

Other crops that have been grown in some parts of the region with success are field peas, rape, sand or hairy vetch, and esparcette. Particularly encouraging results are reported from central Colorado regarding the growing of field peas for forage, and the crop has done well in many other parts of the region. Profitable crops of rape, vetch, and esparcette are reported from Montana and elsewhere.

Millet is more generally grown for hay than any other annual. Common millet and Hungarian are usually preferred for the average uplands. Broom-corn millet is sometimes grown as a grain crop, but yields too lightly for a hay crop where the better varieties can be grown. As a general rule all the millets are used as "catch crops" rather than as regular crops, and as such they fill an important place in northwestern agriculture. They are most commonly grown in the northern part of the region.

NATIVE GRASSES AND FORAGE PLANTS.

There are about 270 species and varieties of grasses known to be indigenous to this region. Naturally a great majority of these are too small or too rare to be of much importance in the production of hay or pasturage. The most valuable species are quite widely distributed, although occasionally a species of but local occurrence may be of considerable importance in its particular locality, as is the case with some of those occurring in the mountains.

The great economic importance of the native grasses is at once apparent when one recalls the many thousands of sheep, cattle, horses, and mules that are raised in this region, and that depend entirely upon the native grasses and forage plants for subsistence for from eight to twelve months of the year. That the quality of the forage afforded is excellent is shown by the fact that most of the vast numbers of fat cattle and sheep annually shipped to the Eastern markets from this region receive no other food than that furnished by the natural meadows and pastures of the ranges.

From the economic point of view the important native grasses of this region may be classed into two groups, namely, meadow grasses and pasture grasses. To be sure, no hard and fast line can be drawn, but as a general thing the best pasture grasses are of little use for hay, and within late years, at least, wherever good hay-producing grasses occur in any great extent, they are fenced off from the open range and preserved for winter forage.

NATIVE MEADOW OR HAY GRASSES.

LOWLAND MEADOWS.

The grasses most abundant in the meadows at the lower altitudes are usually quite different from those which predominate in the mountain meadows, although it is seldom that any sharp line occurs where the strictly mountain grasses begin and the lower valley grasses leave off. The change is rather a gradual one. Hay meadows are almost entirely confined to the valleys of the larger streams, the prairies and hilly country being given over to grazing. Occasionally a rich plateau or "bench" may be found with a sufficient supply of moisture to produce a growth of grass luxuriant enough for hay, but these are rare. The grasses of most importance in the meadows in the lower valleys are wheat-grasses (*Agropyron* spp.), meadow-grasses (*Poa* spp.), manna-grasses (*Panicularia* spp.), sand-grasses or blue-joints (*Calamagrostis* spp.), and wild rye-grasses (*Elymus* spp.).

Of these the wheat-grasses are by far the most valuable. A great many species occur in this region, but there are three which are of special importance as hay-producing grasses. These are Western wheat-grass (*Agropyron spicatum*), known also as Colorado blue-stem, slender wheat-grass (*Agropyron tenerum*) (see fig. 8), and false quack-grass (*Agropyron pseudorepens*). These grasses are very generally distributed over the region, and grow naturally on a great variety of soils. All respond readily to cultivation. Usually all that is necessary to convert a piece of good sagebrush or valley land into a wheat grass meadow is to clear off the brush and large stones, keep off the stock, and water the land. The

Fig. 8.—Slender wheat-grass (*Agropyron tenerum*).

grasses will soon take complete possession. On nearly every well-kept ranch in the eastern Rocky Mountain region can be seen fine natural meadows made in this manner. Western wheat-grass is usually more abundant than either of the other sorts, and it is not an uncommon thing to see a meadow of 40, 80, or more acres composed almost exclusively of this grass. Without irrigation it is rarely possible to cut more than one crop in two years, as the grass requires time to recuperate. Even with irrigation it is seldom possible to obtain good crops for many consecutive years without cutting up the sod to overcome its "hidebound" condition and give opportunity for the growth of new shoots. Under favorable conditions, however, these meadows may yield good crops for a number of years with nothing more than proper watering. Mr. Griffiths reports seeing a meadow of about 40 acres the past season, near Snoma, S. Dak., yielding a crop of about 2 tons of hay per acre, which had afforded a good crop for five consecutive seasons.

In the wet or boggy places in lowland meadows the wheat-grasses are replaced principally by the meadow-grasses and, if the soil is sandy, the sand-grasses or blue joints are often present in considerable quantity. Of these grasses reed meadow- or manna-grass (*Panicularia americana*) (see fig. 9) and nerved manna-grass (*P. nervata*) are common in very wet boggy places unless the soil is too strongly impregnated with alkali, when they are often replaced by alkali meadow-grass (*Puccinellia airoides*). This last grass is usually quite rigid and wiry and grows in close bunches, but furnishes considerable forage in some localities. Often it is about the only grass to be seen among the sedges and rushes of the wet, alkali meadows, and in such places it is more succulent and palatable than when growing in drier situations. It is very abundant in the overirrigated meadows along the Little Laramie River in Wyoming, and is quite widely distributed over the Western plains and throughout the valleys in altitudes below 8,000 feet.

Fig. 9.—Reed meadow-grass (*Panicularia americana*).

The true meadow-grasses (*Poa* spp.) are of much more value generally than those just mentioned. These are most abundant in the moist meadows near the foot of the mountains. Among the valuable kinds are the indigenous forms of Kentucky blue grass (*Poa pratensis*), the "bunch-grasses" (*Poa buckleyana*, *P. laevigata*, and *P. lucida*), Wyoming blue grass (*P. wheeleri*), bench-land spear-grass (*P. arida*), woodland meadow-grass (*P. nemoralis*), Nevada blue grass (*P. nevadensis*), and fowl meadow-grass or false redtop (*P. flava*). Many of these are of as much importance, under present conditions, for pasturage as for hay, but with a proper supply of water all afford good yields of excellent hay. In the valleys Kentucky blue grass, in either its native or introduced form, is perhaps most commonly seen, and is becoming more and more abundant as the country is settled up and the native meadows brought under irrigation.

Of the "bunch-grass" *Poas*, *P. buckleyana* (fig. 10) is apparently the most widely distributed, being, if anything, more common on the dry uplands than in the valleys, and hence perhaps more properly to be regarded as a pasture grass. However, under irrigation it becomes less densely tufted, the leaves are broader and more luxuriant, and the yield of hay is good. Smooth bunch-grass (*P. lævigata*) and pale bunch-grass (*P. lucida*) are more often found in the lowlands and are excellent meadow grasses. They are most abundant in the middle Rocky Mountain region.

Wyoming blue grass is often found with Kentucky blue grass in moist meadows and along banks of streams, but it ascends higher up the mountains, where it is frequently abundant in open pine and spruce woods, sometimes occurring in dry situations, but generally where the soil is well supplied with moisture. It is especially abundant in parts of Wyoming and central Montana, usually occurring at an altitude of from 6,000 to 8,000 or 9,000 feet, but sometimes ascending to 10,000 feet. In the rich moist soil of "burn outs" in pine and spruce woods it makes a magnificent growth.

FIG. 10.—Bunch-grass (*Poa buckleyana*).

Bench-land spear-grass (see fig. 11) is quite generally distributed throughout this region. It usually occurs in rather dry meadows, often in patches of considerable extent, but never forming a close sod, as does Kentucky blue grass. The forage is of poorer quality than that furnished by the latter and the yield is lighter. However, the grass is one of the earliest of the native species and thrives better on dry soil than Kentucky blue grass. Under cultivation it would probably be more valuable for pastures than for meadows.

There are few of the native meadow-grasses that grow naturally under such a wide range of soil and climatic conditions as woodland meadow-grass in its several varieties. It is common in woodlands along the prairie streams, and follows up the valleys into the foothills and mountains, where it becomes an important element in the moist meadows. It also occurs on rocky hills and mountain sides, some of its forms flourishing at an altitude of 10,000 feet, or even more, in Colorado. Some of the forms growing in the rich lowland meadows approach fowl meadow-grass in size and appearance, and afford a large amount of excellent hay.

Nevada blue grass (fig. 12) is more common on the west side of the Continental Divide than on the east, but it is nevertheless sufficiently abundant in the latter region to form an important part of the vegetation in many of the natural meadows. It occurs as far east as the Pine Ridge of Nebraska and the Black Hills of South Dakota, but is most abundant in the valleys among the foothills and mountains. Some forms of it grow on rather dry soil in open woodlands and on rocky mountain sides. It prefers rich soil with a medium supply of moisture and does well under irrigation. Under favorable conditions it makes an excellent growth of leaves, and yields a large amount of hay compared with most of the native species of *Poa*. It is rarely found above an altitude of 8,000 or 9,000 feet in this region.

FIG. 11.—Bench-land spear-grass (*Poa arida*).

Fowl meadow-grass is not as abundant in the immediate vicinity of the mountains as it is farther to the eastward, but nevertheless is found quite plentifully in certain localities. It occurs most frequently along streams about the edges of thickets, and on moist banks and bottom lands subject to overflow in the early part of the season. For such places it is a valuable grass, making a good yield under conditions that would "drown out" most of the common grasses. It is much more valuable for hay than for pasturage. In some localities this grass is called false redtop.

The sand-grasses or blue joints found in the meadows are remarkable for their abundance of long root-leaves and the consequent large yield of hay, which is usually of an excellent quality. One of the most widely distributed species is the common blue joint (*Calamagrostis canadensis*), locally known as false or native redtop. This grass is often very abundant in moist, sandy river bottoms, and some of its many forms ascend well up into the mountains. It has been cultivated with good success and is worthy of extended trial in the Northwest.

Sand-grass or yellow-top (*Calamagrostis americana*) is also well distributed throughout this region. It is most commonly found along the sandy banks of streams, ponds, and lakes, often (especially along sloughs) forming a well-defined "yellow-top" zone of vegetation, noticeable from a considerable distance because of the characteristic color of the grass. It seems to thrive better in alkali soils than its relatives, and is generally confined to comparatively low altitudes.

Big sand-grass (*Calamovilfa longifolia*), although common on the plains and in the valleys throughout, is not so valuable as the preceding species because of the very coarse and fibrous nature of the forage which it produces. It is most commonly found in dry, sandy swales and on sandy hillsides, and in the bad lands and other dry districts, where the better grasses are scarce, it is often plentiful. In such localities it is regarded as a valuable grass, and is used for hay.

There are several of the wild rye-grasses that occur in suffi-

Fig. 12.—Nevada blue grass (*Poa nevadensis*).

cient quantities to be of importance in the vegetation of the native meadows. All are most abundant as a rule in rich, open, rather dry meadows and on hillsides, and are rather coarse, harsh plants, affording considerable hay of an average quality. The kinds of most importance are common wild-rye (*Elymus canadensis*), Macoun's rye-grass (*E. macounii*), and giant rye-grass (*E. condensatus*). The first of these is the most generally distributed, and is probably the most valuable, although the second, which is also quite common, is a finer grass and produces a better quality of hay.

Giant rye-grass is a tall, coarse species, growing in large clumps, found in sandy or gravelly soil of meadows and hillsides. It is too harsh and woody to be relished by stock, and is seldom eaten except when young, or in winter, when other forage is scarce or when the snow is deep. Owing to its habit of growing in such dense bunches it is difficult to cut for hay. However, when better grasses are scarce it is frequently cut early, and the hay is said to be of fair quality. When a meadow becomes thickly seeded to this grass and is cut or burned closely for several seasons a fairly even sod is produced, and such a meadow is of considerable value, particularly when, as is usually the case, the better grasses can not be grown because of adverse soil or climatic conditions. Such meadows are much more common on the west side of the Continental Divide than on the east. During the summer of 1896 a number of such meadows were seen in southwestern Montana and eastern Idaho, and in 1897 several were seen in north-western Wyoming. This grass usually ripens a large amount of seed, and stock gets a great deal of nourishment by eating the seed-heads in fall and winter. Horses are said to be particularly fond of them.

On the eastern edge of this region Virginian lyme-grass (*Elymus virginicus*) is quite common in some localities, but is more valuable for early pasturage than for hay.

Among other native grasses that may be mentioned as of value in native meadows, but which only occasionally occupy any prominent place in them, are bearded wheat-grass (*Agropyron richardsoni*), in rather dry meadows; the cord-grasses (*Spartina cynosuroides* and *S. gracilis*), in sloughs and low places, the latter in alkali situations, particularly; slough-grass or wild timothy (*Beckmannia erucœformis*), along sloughs and irrigation ditches and in wet meadows, becoming very abundant in many parts of the region; and reed canary-grass (*Phalaris arundinacea*), abundant in places, and particularly valuable in wet meadow lands and sloughs.

MOUNTAIN MEADOWS.

The mountain meadows, so numerous in portions of this region, differ considerably in the composition of their vegetation from those of the lower valleys and plains discussed in the previous pages. Here the true meadow-grasses form the predominating element, replacing the wheat-grasses of the lower meadows; the brome-grasses (*Bromus* spp.), seldom seen at the lower altitudes, are here abundant; the tussock-grasses (*Deschampsia* spp.) are plentiful everywhere in wet, boggy situations; and the blue joints (*Calamagrostis* spp.), alpine timothy (*Phleum alpinum*), mountain foxtail (*Alopecurus occidentalis*), the wild oat-grasses (*Danthonia* spp.), rough-leafed bent (*Agrostis asperifolia*), and red fescue (*Festuca rubra*) are all valuable members of the vegetation of these meadows.

Of the blue grasses (*Poa* spp.) several of those mentioned in the foregoing discussion are common in the mountain meadows, namely, Wyoming blue grass (see fig. 13), smooth bunch-grass, Nevada blue grass, and woodland meadow-grass. In the higher altitudes alpine blue grass (*Poa alpina*) and mountain meadow-grass (*Poa leptocoma*) are the predominating species. An interesting thing in connection with the distribution of these two grasses was observed in northern Wyoming the past season. In the Bear Lodge range, in northeastern Wyoming, alpine blue grass was frequently met, and it was also very abundant in the mountains at the head of Meeteetse Creek in the northwestern part of the State, but extended search failed to reveal any of this grass in the Big Horn Mountains in the north central part of the State and nearly midway between the other two localities. Mountain meadow-grass was very abundant in the Big Horn Mountains, and was also found in the mountains at the head of Meeteetse Creek, but was not seen in the northeastern part of the State. Alpine blue grass is most abundant in sandy or gravelly soil near the streams, and mountain meadow-grass prefers cold, wet, boggy meadows and mountain sides.

Alpine timothy is very widely distributed at the higher elevations in the Rocky Mountain region. It is quite abundant in the Black Hills above 6,000 feet. In the Big Horn Mountains it vies with tussock-grass for first place in many of the meadows at 7,000

Fig. 13.—Wyoming blue grass (*Poa wheeleri*).

to 8,000 feet, particularly on the western side of the range, where it is much more abundant than on the eastern slope. In central Montana it is most plentiful at and above 6,500 feet, rarely occurring below 6,000 feet, the ordinary limit for common timothy. It is rarely found below 9,000 feet in Colorado, except, perhaps, in the northern part of the State, but is plentiful up to 13,000 feet. Hay made from this grass is highly prized by ranchmen, especially for horses.

Mountain foxtail (fig. 14), which is also sometimes called mountain timothy, has much the appearance of true mountain or alpine timothy, but is usually more robust and of a softer texture and produces a better looking hay, much like that from the cultivated meadow foxtail (*Alopecurus pratensis*), which this grass resembles in habit of growth. Although found throughout the Rocky Mountain region, and having similar altitudinal limits, it is much less common as a rule than alpine timothy. It is abundant in the rich, moist meadows of the Spanish Basin and elsewhere in southwestern Montana, and makes a remarkably luxuriant growth, frequently reaching a height of three or four feet, and is one of the most promising of the native grasses for cultivation in meadows at the higher altitudes.

Several of the native brome-grasses are of great value in the native meadows at an altitude of from 5,000 to 8,000 feet in Wyoming and Montana and from 6,000 to 9,500 in Colorado. The most valuable of these brome-grasses are short-awned brome (*Bromus breviaristatus*) (see fig. 15) and Western brome (*Bromus pumpellianus*). Both are coarse-growing perennials and occur throughout the Rocky Mountain region, chiefly in the rather dry valleys and "parks;" the former selecting the moister situations and the latter the drier ones. Although they are often found growing together, Western brome-grass seems to have a somewhat higher altitudinal limit, its point of best development usually ranging from 500 to 1,000 feet above that of short-awned brome. The latter is occasionally abundant down as low as 4,000 feet in central Montana, while the former is but rarely found at that altitude. In northern Wyoming short-awned brome is most abundant at from 5,000 to 7,000 feet and Western brome at from 6,000 to 8,000. Both of these grasses have been cultivated in some parts of the Northwest with success and promise to be valuable for meadows at high altitudes. Western brome has very much the same appearance and habit of growth as

FIG. 14.—Mountain Foxtail (*Alopecurus occidentalis*).

the recently introduced smooth or Hungarian brome which is being grown with such excellent success in the semiarid West and Northwest.

Tussock-grass (*Deschampsia cœspitosa*) is perhaps the most abundant and widely distributed grass in the native meadows of the Rocky Mountain region. It has a very wide altitudinal range. For example, it is abundant in wet meadows in the Gallatin Valley about Bozeman, Mont., at an altitude of about 4,000 feet, and ascends to above the timber line in the mountains on either side of the valley. On account of its tufted habit of growth it does not form an even sod, and hence does not make a good meadow by itself. In most instances, however, it is accompanied by other grasses, such as the true meadow-grasses, redtop and blue joint, which fill in the spaces between the tufts, making a fairly good meadow sod. Some observers have reported this grass as of no practical value for either hay or pasturage, but such statements are not borne out by the reports of our field agents nor by the opinions advanced by the ranchers.

While neither the yield nor the quality of the forage is equal to that obtained from timothy or redtop, there can be no doubt that the grass fills an important place among the native meadow and pasture grasses of this region. It flourishes in wet,

Fig. 15.—Short-awned Brome-grass (*Bromus breviaristatus*): *a*, the floret seen from the side; *b*, palea; *c*, joint of the rachilla; *d*, grain; *e*, lower portion of pistil, showing lodicules; *f*, young seed or grain.

boggy places where many of the better grasses can not grow, and by its dense tufts of tough fibrous roots helps to convert these bogs into usable meadow lands. Moreover, continued mowing and pasturing have the effect of reducing these tufts materially, so that with a few other grasses to act as fillers a comparatively even sod is produced. Such a condition of things may be seen in many of the mountain valleys, as, for example, in the valley of the Little Laramie River near Sheep

Mountain. In the varieties of tussock-grass growing in the higher altitudes the leaves become considerably reduced, and, of course, produce little forage of any sort, but the varieties growing in the meadows at from 4,000 to 6,500 feet develop a much greater leafage and afford a large amount of hay and pasturage.

A form of red fescue is not uncommon in the moist meadows at from 4,000 to 9,000 feet altitude in the northern part of the Rocky Mountain region, and is of much value for hay in some localities. It seldom forms tufts of any size, spreads by means of very slender underground stems, and is usually found mixed with other grasses. It is quite abundant in the Spanish Basin and elsewhere in southwestern Montana, and also in the Big Horn and Shoshone mountains in Wyoming.

Rough-leafed bent occurs naturally in wet, boggy meadows and along banks of streams and ditches. The best hay-producing forms occur at elevations of from 4,000 to 6,000, or occasionally 7,000, feet. This grass produces an abundant leafage, much more than the common redtop, and also produces a large amount of seed—two things very desirable in a grass for cultivation. In the wild state it seems to be even more hardy than redtop, and while flourishing best with plenty of water it will, nevertheless, endure considerable drought when once firmly established. It is quite an important

FIG. 16.—Rocky Mountain oat-grass (*Dantho-nia intermedia*).

element in the native meadows in portions of northern Wyoming and central and southern Montana, and is perhaps more common on the west side of the Continental Divide than on the east. As ordinarily seen in the natural condition, rough-leafed bent has a closely tufted habit of growth, but when thickly seeded, as when in cultivation or occasionally in native meadows when conditions are favorable, this habit is largely lost, and a fairly even sod is formed. Its good qualities as a meadow grass commend it to those experimenting with our native species. It will doubtless be found to be better adapted for meadows at higher altitudes than most of the common so-called tame grasses.

There are several of the oat-grasses found in greater or less abundance in the meadows and "parks" of the mountains and foothills of this region. The most important are Californian oat-grass (*Danthonia californica*), Rocky Mountain oat-grass (*Danthonia intermedia*) (see fig. 16), and Parry's oat-grass (*Danthonia parryi*).

As a rule these oat-grasses occur naturally in rather dry meadows and on mountain sides, Californian oat-grass being more inclined to seek moist situations than either of the others. It is the largest of the native oat-grasses, reaching a height of 3 feet under favorable conditions, and is also the most abundant Northwestern species. In northern Wyoming and Montana it forms a considerable portion of the meadow vegetation at from 5,500 to 8,000 feet. It is occasionally found as low as 5,000 feet, but is most abundant at from 6,000 to 7,000 feet. On rich, irrigated meadows it makes a very fine growth. It is rarely found as far south as Colorado, where it is replaced by Parry's oat-grass.

Rocky Mountain oat-grass is often found growing along with Californian oat-grass; but it is a smaller plant, preferring rather drier soil and having a somewhat higher altitudinal range—seldom occurring below 7,000 feet, abundant at 8,000 to 10,000 feet, and ascending to 11,000 feet or even 12,500 feet in Colorado. It is probably of more value for pasturage than for hay.

Parry's oat-grass is most abundant in the park region of Colorado, but also occurs in southern Wyoming. Although occurring naturally in rather dry meadows and on mountain sides, it makes a fine growth under irrigation and is occasionally found in some quantity in timothy meadows. It has a much more tufted habit of growth than Californian oat-grass and its altitudinal range—from 7,000 to 10,000 feet—corresponds very well to that of its more northern relative. Although of local occurrence it is abundant in places, sometimes almost completely occupying the open woods and parks in the mountains of central Colorado.

The blue joints are usually conspicuous elements in the vegetation of the moister mountain meadows. They are the chief grasses in many of the deer parks in the higher mountains, and are particularly abundant in the wet, boggy, open aspen thickets so frequently found in the Northwest. There are about a half-dozen species which are found in sufficient quantities to be of importance as forage producers. By far the most abundant is mountain blue-joint (*Calamagrostis canadensis acuminata*), a near relative of the common blue joint, which it replaces in the higher altitudes. It produces a large amount of excellent hay in the wet, sandy or gravelly valleys along the mountain streams, and usually occurs at an altitude of from 5,000 to 8,000 feet in the North, but ascends to 10,000 or rarely to 11,000 feet in Colorado. In northern Wyoming and central and southern Montana it makes an enormous development in the rich, moist soil of some of the mountain parks, frequently covering areas several acres in extent with a dense growth, reaching a height of 3½ or 4 feet.

Northern blue joint or Langsdorff's reed-bent (*Calamagrostis langsdorffii*) is often found growing along with mountain blue joint and has a similar range, but is much less, abundant and has rather higher altitudinal limits. In localities where it is plentiful it is highly prized by stockmen, by whom it is often called "purpletop" on account of the prevailing color of the inflorescence. It is much more common to the northward, being but rarely found as far south as Colorado, and then only in the higher mountains.

Other blue joints deserving special mention are Scribner's blue joint (*Calamagrostis scribneri*) and Suksdorf's blue-joint (*C. suksdorfii*). Both are northern in distribution, the latter being found in this region only in central and western Montana and most abundant west of the Continental Divide, and the former reaching down into central or rarely into southern Wyoming and Colorado. Both have an altitudinal range of about 3,000 feet, seldom occurring below 5,000 feet or above 8,000 feet in Wyoming and Montana. Suksdorf's blue joint, although reaching its best development in the moist land of the valleys, is often found on the drier ridges and mountain sides.

NATIVE PASTURE GRASSES.

Naturally much the greater portion of the grass land is used for grazing. At the present time nearly all the land not under irrigation is used for this purpose. This includes by far the larger part of the upland prairies, the bad lands, the broken foothill country, and the accessible mountainous country.

Some of these pasture lands, notably those in the mountains and higher foothills, can be used during only a portion of the year, but the remainder are grazed through the entire year. In some localities certain portions of the range are protected during the growing season in order that the grass may make a good growth and furnish forage for fall and winter grazing. Sometimes the stock is kept from these areas by fencing, but often the ranchmen, by common consent, keep the stock on other ranges during the summer, and bring it to the protected areas only when forced to do so by the approach of severe winter weather. In localities where the meadow lands and winter pastures are fenced in, the open range is usually in very bad condition. Every ranchman is eager to get his "share" of the open and free range, and naturally turns out all his stock during the summer. As a result, the grasses and better forage plants are eaten up or trampled into the ground before the end of the season. What wonder that the grasses are dying out on the open range! The wonder is that they have survived as long as they have. During the past season, while making wagon trips through the Belle Fourche and Big Horn Basin countries, it was often necessary to drive many miles in order to find sufficient pasturage for the team. All the grass lands not under fence were picked bare in July and August, and it was impossible to get feed along the trail except by obtaining permission of the ranchers to camp inside the inclosures. Of course the grasses are being preserved within the fenced areas, but these compose but a relatively small part of the total pasture lands, and the get-all-you-can system is rapidly and certainly ruining the open range. In parts of the range region the scarcity of stock during the past few years, together with a few favorable growing seasons, has allowed the grasses to recuperate somewhat, but already the stockmen are beginning to increase their herds in order to be able to take advantage of the anticipated rise in prices of beef cattle, mutton, and wool, and there is danger that those lands not already overstocked will soon be so unless something can be done to convince these stockmen of the shortsightedness of such a policy.

In the higher foothills and mountains the pasturage is generally in good condition—much better than on the prairies. There are two principal reasons for this. In the first place, there is usually a good supply of moisture, and in the second place, the lands can be grazed during only a portion of the year on account of the heavy snowfall. As the lands can be grazed for but four or five months of the year at the outside, there is a long period during the early part of the season when the grasses make a considerable growth, so that they are already well along in the season's development, sometimes maturing seed, before grazing begins.

GRASSES OF THE PLAINS.

Out on the open ranges of the plains, however, there are few localities in which the pasturage is anything like as good as in former years. Leading stockmen from nearly all parts of the plains region estimate that the stock-carrying capacity of the pasture lands has been reduced on the average from 40 to 50 per cent in the last ten or fifteen years. The real reason for this is overstocking. The real stock-carrying capacity of a given area of pasture lands is the amount of stock that can safely be grazed on it during a dry or unfavorable season; and if these lands are to be kept in proper condition this limit should never be exceeded except perhaps temporarily during particularly favorable seasons; and the number of stock should be reduced as soon as it is seen that the grasses are being grazed too closely. Under the present system, or rather lack of system, of controlling the open grazing lands, it is hardly to be expected that the ranchman will do otherwise than to continue to try to get his "share" of the forage on the open range, and in so doing will continue to add to its already overburdened condition.

There are many thousands of acres of the public lands in this region that are of more value for grazing than for any other purpose, and in view of their importance and of the great danger of permanent injury resulting from the present methods of grazing it would seem urgent that some rational system of controlling them should be devised and adopted at once.

All the native grasses are grazed by stock to a greater or less extent, but many kinds are too small to afford much forage; others are too coarse and woody, or otherwise unpalatable, to be of much value; and still others, while affording nutritious forage, are of most value for hay, and have been considered in the preceding pages of this report under the discussion of the native meadow-grasses.

The principal pasture grasses of the dry plains region are the gramas (*Bouteloua* spp.), buffalo-grass (*Bulbilis dactyloides*), wheat grasses, already discussed under meadow-grasses, prairie June-grass (*Koeleria cristata*), and needle-grasses (*Stipa* spp.). Other grasses of considerable value for grazing, but of more or less local distribution, are Indian millet (*Eriocoma cuspidata*), rush-grasses (*Sporobolus* spp.), Montana sand-grass (*Calamagrostis montanensis*), salt-grass (*Distichlis spicata*), and several of the bunch-grasses and wild ryes already mentioned.

There are three gramas found in this region, and all are valuable pasture grasses. The best, and by far the most abundant, is blue grama (*Bouteloua oligostachya*). (See fig. 17.) It is one of the most generally distributed grasses of the prairies, and also occurs in considerable quantities on the higher bench lands and mesas, in the foothills, and in dry soil here and there in the lower mountain valleys. Everywhere it is regarded as an exceedingly valuable grass for both summer and winter pasturage, but particularly for the latter, vying with buffalo-grass for first place. At the present time it is probably of greater actual value on account of its more general occurrence, greater yield of forage, and greater ability to hold possession of the soil under excessive pasturing and extreme drought. In the rather loose, sandy soil, so common to the prairies of this region, blue grama forms closely sodded areas of varying extent which, on account of the purplish color of the foliage, stand out in strong contrast to the prevailing

Fig. 17.—Blue grama (*Bouteloua oligostachya*): *a*, empty glumes of a spikelet; *b*, spikelet with the empty glumes removed.

pale color of the remaining grass vegetation. Often these areas may be found alternating with similar areas of the much paler buffalo-grass, and the checkerboard appearance thus given to the prairie is peculiarly striking. Although primarily a pasture grass, blue grama, under favorable conditions of soil and moisture, makes a fine growth of leafage sufficient to afford a good yield of hay of a very fine quality. Under ordinary conditions, however, this grass cures so well on the ground that stockmen prefer to use it for winter pasturage rather than go to the trouble of putting up the hay.

Black grama (*Bouteloua hirsuta*) is much more local in distribution than blue grama, to which it is very similar in appearance and habit of growth. It is confined largely to rather limited areas on sandy or gravelly knolls and hillsides, and is valuable chiefly because it thrives in these poor soils, furnishing considerable pasturage where but few other grasses can do more than simply exist.

The third grama found in this region that deserves special mention is tall or side-oats grama (*Bouteloua curtipendula*). (See fig. 18.) It is a larger grass than either of the foregoing, and, while occurring throughout, is more abundant in the rich prairie soil of the eastern portion of the region. It produces a fine growth of

Fig. 18.—Tall or side-oats grama (*Bouteloua curtipendula*): *a*, one of the short spikes; *b*, a spikelet; *c*, a spikelet with the outer empty glumes removed.

long, slender leaves and on good soil makes a good yield of hay. In Nebraska and the Dakotas, where this grass is very abundant, it is regarded as of more value for hay than for pasturage, as it yields well, and the tough, rather harsh leaves are more readily eaten by stock as hay than when in the fresh state. In the principal range region, however, the grass is seldom present in the meadows in much quantity, and on the drier soils the growth is not sufficient for hay; but it cures well on the ground and is readily eaten by range stock which are more accustomed to feeding on harsh herbage.

There is no other grass which has a reputation for excellence for both summer and winter pasturage equal to that of buffalo-grass. However, not all of the praise bestowed upon this grass really belongs to it, for the gramas are often confused with it, and to them, particularly to blue grama, belongs much of the credit given to buffalo-grass in many parts of the range region. In the minds of many ranchmen "buffalo-grass" includes blue grama and black grama as well as the true buffalo-grass (*Bulbilis dactyloides*), while in the minds of others grama or "grammer," as it is often pronounced, includes all three.

However, there is no doubt of the great value of the true buffalo-grass for pasturage. That it is one of the most palatable of native grasses is shown by the fact that, with plenty of other grasses on every hand, stock will keep it eaten close to the ground, and this is probably the reason that it is one of the first grasses to be killed out in over-stocked ranges. It is reported to have practically disappeared from many places where it was formerly one of the commonest species, but while this is no doubt true of some localities, it is certainly not true of all. Examination has shown that it is still quite abundant in some of these localities, but is easily overlooked, as it is kept grazed so closely that it is seldom able to make enough development to show its characteristic habit of growth, much less to bloom and mature seed.

The wheat-grasses usually furnish a larger percentage of the pasturage on the prairies than is generally supposed. The most valuable varieties for grazing are provided with underground stems or root-stocks, which run along a short distance below the surface and at frequent intervals send up erect branches, either bearing only tufts of leaves or more rarely producing "heads." When too closely grazed, or during unfavorable seasons, much of the growth of the plant is made by these underground stems and very few, if any, fertile branches are developed. On this account many people have an idea that these grasses grow only once in every two or three years, when as a matter of fact the actual yield of forage may be almost as much for an "off" year as for any other. Although regarded primarily as meadow or hay grasses, the wheat-grasses furnish a large part of the pasturage throughout the entire range region, and on the more strongly alkaline soils are often the only grasses of any value to be found at all.

The needle-grasses (*Stipa* spp.) are among the most conspicuous members of the grass vegetation of the plains and lower mountains and foothills. All produce a relatively large amount of leafage, which makes an excellent quality of forage. During the late summer, when the seed is maturing, some of the needle-grasses cause much trouble and often severe injury to stock, particularly to sheep, as the sharp-pointed needles or "spears" work into the flesh of the animals, making painful sores and sometimes causing the death of the animal. In some of the best forage-producing species the "spears" are very blunt, and hence do little or no damage. Where the range is kept closely grazed the plants seldom seed in sufficient quantity to be troublesome. As soon as the seed ripens the "spears" fall and work into the soil, so that these grasses can be used for hay or late grazing.

The common needle-grass (*Stipa comata*) of this region is valuable for both hay and pasturage. On poor rocky or gravelly soils, where it is one of the characteristic species (see fig. 19), it affords a large amount of pasturage, and on the rich prairie soils it makes a good yield of hay which is considered by many ranchmen to be equal in quality to "blue-stem" or wheat-grass hay. Here in the range region it takes the place of porcupine-grass (*Stipa spartea*), so abundant in the Lower Missouri Valley region, but which only occurs in any considerable quantity along

Fig. 19.—A bit of the "range" in N. E. Wyoming. (Photographed by David Griffiths.)

the eastern limits of the range. In some parts of the range, as for example in some localities of central and northern Wyoming, the common needle-grass sometimes composes the entire grass vegetation of the sage-brush prairies.

Another of the needle-grasses common in some of its many forms in this region is that most commonly known as feather bunch-grass (*Stipa viridula*). This is usually found in rather dry sandy soil, and forms dense tufted masses of leaves and stems, which afford good grazing. On account of its very blunt-pointed "spears" it seldom does any damage to stock and, as it endures close feeding well, it is one of the most desirable of the needle-grasses for grazing. Because of its densely tufted habit of growth and less luxuriant production of root leaves it is of less value for hay than common needle-grass. Nelson's needle-grass (*Stipa nelsoni*) and purple-top needle-grass (*Stipa minor*) are also of value for pasturage, but both belong more properly, perhaps, to the higher altitudes. On the Big Horn ranges, at about 8,000 feet altitude, purple-top needle-grass is an important pasture grass and is also frequently cut for hay.

Sleepy-grass (*Stipa vaseyi*) is quite abundant in the southern part of the eastern Rocky Mountain region. It takes its common name from the fact that in some localities it is thought to have a narcotic effect upon stock eating it. It is a coarse-growing grass, and the forage could hardly be very palatable in any event. However, in times of scarcity of pasturage it is quite closely grazed, in central Colorado at least, but whether with any ill effects has not been definitely ascertained. It is possible that the narcotic principle is not everywhere produced in injurious quantities.

One of the best early pasture grasses on the range is prairie June-grass (*Koeleria cristata*). (See fig. 20.) It is widely distributed, flourishes on a variety of soils, and is one of the earliest grasses to afford pasturage on the prairies. It has a tufted habit of

Fig. 20.—Prairie June-grass (*Koeleria cristata*): *a*, empty glumes; *b*, the two florets raised above the empty glumes.

growth and seldom exceeds a foot in height on the dry prairies, but in moist valleys it frequently reaches 2 feet or more and affords an excellent quality of hay. It matures its seed early and then dries up, furnishing but little fresh pasturage afterwards unless well watered. It usually seeds heavily. Stockmen regard it as one of the most valuable native pasture grasses because of its earliness and palatability. To many it is known as wild or prairie timothy, because of its external resemblance to the common cultivated timothy.

One of the most common and valuable "bunch-grasses" on the plains is *Poa buckleyana*. It is most abundant on the high elevated plains and bench lands nearer the mountains, and is usually accompanied by prairie June-grass, blue grama, and some of the wheat-grasses. It is not as early as prairie June-grass, but affords a larger amount of forage and is much better for winter pasturage. It has a very wide distribution in the Rocky Mountain region and is represented by a great variety of forms, some of which, as already mentioned in another connection, are valuable hay producers.

In poor sandy soil, or in that containing a large percentage of alkali, the rush-grasses (*Sporobolus* spp.) are important pasture grasses. They are all rather harsh and unpalatable and are valuable chiefly because they thrive in soil that will produce none of the better grasses. When forage is plentiful, stock will not eat them to any great extent, and the plants soon become tough and woody, but during seasons of scarcity these grasses are, like others, kept closely grazed throughout the season and are tenderer and more palatable. During the past season a number of extensive pastures were observed in the Big Horn Basin composed almost exclusively of fine-top rush-grass or salt-grass (*Sporobolus airoides*). (See fig. 21.) These pastures were in alkali bottoms and old lake beds, and were almost the only grass-covered areas of any consequence in that locality. They were grazed by horses principally, and were reported to be improving with continual pasturing. This grass is most abundant in the southern portion of the region, though occurring throughout.

FIG. 21.—Fine-top salt-grass (*Sporobolus airoides*).

Among other rush-grasses of general occurrence in this region are rough-leafed salt-grass (*Sporobolus asperifolius*), a characteristic "badland" grass; sand rush-grass (*S. cryptandrus*), often abundant in sandy prairies and river bottoms; and prairie rush-grass (*S. depauperatus*). There are two forms of the last occurring in this region; one found chiefly in dry soil of prairies and hillsides, too small to be of much value for forage, and the other in moist, more or less alkaline bottom land, tall and slender and producing a greater amount of forage.

Another grass abundant throughout this region in strongly alkaline soils, but of little value except in times of scarcity of forage, is the common salt- or alkali-grass (*Distichlis spicata*). (See fig. 22.) Although often producing a great deal of leafage, it is harsh and unpalatable and is refused by stock as long as other grasses are to be obtained. Sheep eat it more readily than other stock. It is abundant in the bad-land regions, and, as better grasses are usually scarce there, it is sometimes cut for hay. In localities where the land is becoming "alkalied" through improper irrigation, this grass is spreading rapidly and often becomes quite a pest.

Montana sand-grass (*Calamagrostis montanensis*) is the only representative of this genus that is of much importance as a pasture grass on the dry prairies and foothills. Its distribution is rather local, but where it does occur in any quantity it is a valuable grass. It thrives on sterile, sandy prairies and hillsides and produces a large amount of leaves. It cures well on the ground, and hence affords good winter pasturage. It has not been reported south of the Big Horn Basin, in Wyoming, where it was found the past season in considerable abundance, particularly along the Gray Bull River, on the west side of the basin. It was first observed in quantity at about 5,000 feet altitude, growing on dry, sandy flats and bluffs, continued plentiful up to about 7,000 feet and then gradually became less and less common, disappearing entirely at 8,000 feet.

FIG. 22.—Salt-grass (*Distichlis spicata*).

GRASSES OF THE FOOTHILLS AND MOUNTAINS.

The grasses of the lower foothills differ but little from those of the plains. The sod-forming species become more confined to the valleys and the "bunch" grasses become more and more conspicuous on the bluffs and hillsides. As the higher foothills and mountains are approached, however, changes in the grass flora become apparent. The gramas and wheat-grasses of the plains are replaced by "bunch-grasses" of various kinds, sheep fescue (*Festuca ovina*), and mountain wheat-grass (*Agropyron violaceum*); brome-grasses become more abundant; the common needle-grass, porcupine-grass and feather bunch-grass give way to Tweedy's needle-grass (*Stipa tweedyi*), Nelson's needle-grass (*S. nelsoni*), and purple-top needle-grass (*S. minor*); wild oat-grasses, meadow or spear-grasses, and tussock-grass become plentiful; and mountain blue joint takes the place of common blue joint and yellow-top.

In the dry soils of the higher foothills and mountains the most important pasture grasses are the "bunch grasses" and the oat-grasses. The former term is a very general one, and as used on the range includes a great many different kinds of grasses. For example, in Colorado "bunch-grass" probably most often means one of the fescues (*Festuca scabrella*), more properly called buffalo bunch-grass; in Wyoming and Montana the term is probably most often applied to the three *Poas* mentioned under the discussion of meadow-grasses, but is also often applied to certain of the fescues, as sheep fescue—often also called "deer grass"—and King's fescue (*Festuca kingii*) (see fig. 23), the northern

Fig. 23.—King's fescue (*Festuca kingii*).

representative of buffalo bunch-grass. Some of the wheat-grasses (*Agropyron divergens* and *A. vaseyi*) are also "bunch-grasses," but as a rule some modification of the term is used in designating them, as wire bunch-grass or bunch wheat-grass. All the above-mentioned grasses are valuable as forage producers and are widely distributed, most of them occurring over all or at least a large portion of the eastern Rocky Mountain region. In the higher altitudes sheep fescue, the bunch-grass *Poas*, and the wild-oat-grasses furnish most of the pasturage in the dry parks and open places. The mountain form of prairie June-grass (*Koeleria cristata*) is often sufficiently abundant to form a large part of the pasturage in such places.

In the moister soils the pasturage is furnished by the grasses mentioned in the discussion of mountain meadows, supplemented by various additional species of more local occurrence or of less vigorous growth, and hence of less value as forage producers.

Among such additional species might be mentioned downy oat-grass (*Trisetum subspicatum molle*), American oat-grass (*Avena americana*), and a variety of Californian oat-grass (*Danthonia californica unispicata*). The first is an abundant and widely distributed grass, flourishing in a variety of soils, but most commonly found in rather moist open woodlands and edges of thickets. American oat-grass is rather local in distribution, is seldom found below an altitude of 6,000 feet in Montana and Wyoming or about 7,500 in Colorado, and is most abundant in the upper part of the eastern Rocky Mountain region. It usually occurs in rather dry bottoms or on hillsides, and when plentiful affords much good forage. The variety of Californian oat-grass is smaller than the species and is generally found on dry ridges and hillsides, while the species occurs in rather moist meadows. It is quite abundant in portions of Wyoming and western Montana and is regarded as a good pasture grass, to some extent taking the place, in high altitudes, occupied by blue grama on the plains.

NATIVE CLOVERS, VETCHES, AND LUPINES.

The eastern Rocky Mountain region is well supplied with native leguminous plants, many of which are of great value for hay and pasturage. Some are unpalatable and are seldom eaten by stock, and a few are injurious when eaten in any considerable quantity, due to certain poisons or other active principles contained in them. In the three States included in this report there are more than a dozen native clovers, eight or ten native vetches and vetchlings, at least fifty milk-vetches or rattleweeds, two bush-peas, a dozen or more lupines, and a host of other legumes.

THE CLOVERS.

The native clovers are found chiefly in the mountains and at comparatively high altitudes. Some of them are too rare and others too small to be of much value for forage, but the majority are valuable, and four or five are of sufficient importance to warrant careful experimentation as to their possible use as cultivated crops. From their appearance and thriftiness under natural conditions or in irrigated native meadows it would certainly seem probable that several of them would prove of great value for cultivation, especially in the higher altitudes, where alfalfa and the common clovers can not be successfully grown.

Among the most important of these native clovers are Beckwith's clover (*Trifolium beckwithii*), long-stalked clover (*T. longipes*), mountain red clover (*T. megacephalum*), Parry's clover (*T. parryi*), silky dwarf clover (*T. dasyphyllum*), woolly-headed clover (*T. eriocephalum*), and Hayden's clover (*T. haydeni*). Of these, the first three are probably the most valuable. Beckwith's clover has the lowest altitudinal limit. It is abundant in rich meadows in some localities in southwestern Montana at an altitude of about 5,000 feet, and extends as far to the eastward as the Sioux Valley in South Dakota, where it is frequently abundant, though rather local in distribution. It makes a very fine growth in the rich irrigated meadows in Montana, and is regarded as a valuable hay plant. In South Dakota it is found along rather dry swales and creek bottoms and affords a considerable amount of pasturage, and under more favorable conditions becomes large enough to be cut for hay. It seems to endure drought quite well, better than the common red clover, and is well worthy of experimentation. On account of the similarity of the flower heads to those of the common clover, it is sometimes called "wild red clover."

Long-stalked clover is one of the commonest of the clovers native to this region, and has a wide distribution, extending from southern Colorado along the Rocky Mountains to British America and west to the Pacific Slope. It is seldom found below an altitude corresponding to 6,000 feet in southern Colorado. It is at its best near the uppermost limit for alfalfa, and is often found in quantity up to 9,000 feet altitude. It is a slender, narrow-leafed plant, usually a foot or more in height, with pale, cream-colored or purplish flowers. It is highly prized as a forage

Fig. 24.—Mountain red clover (*Trifolium megacephalum*).

plant by stockmen, by whom the pale-flowered variety is sometimes called "wild white clover." It makes a fine growth in irrigated meadows and deserves to be given a trial under cultivation.

Woolly-headed clover has much the appearance of long-stalked clover, and occurs in similar situations, but seems to have a more limited distribution, and is chiefly confined to the region west of the Continental Divide.

Mountain red clover (see fig. 24) is one of the most robust-growing native sorts found in the Rocky Mountain region. The flower heads are large and showy, and the leaves are composed of from five to seven leaflets, instead of three, as is the case with the other clovers of the

region. It produces stout, deep-growing roots, and has many other qualities commending it to the attention of the experimenter. Like the preceding, it is most widely distributed on the west side of the Continental Divide.

The other clovers mentioned in the preceding list are all rather small and are of especial value only as pasturage. The most important are: Parry's clover, generally distributed in the central Rocky Mountain region, and most abundant at an altitude of from 10,000 to 13,000 feet; silky dwarf clover, likewise occurring in the central Rocky Mountain region, but with lower altitudinal limits and growing on drier soil than Parry's clover; and Hayden's clover, occurring in moist soil from Wyoming north along the mountains at an altitude of from 7,000 to 10,200 feet.

All the clovers mentioned in the preceding pages are perennials. There are only two or three species of the annual clovers native to the region. Annual red clover (*Trifolium involucratum*) is widely distributed and is by far the most valuable of the annual sorts. Few-flowered clover (*T. pauciflorum*) is occasionally met with, and it is likely that small-headed clover (*T. microcephalum*) may occur in western Colorado and southwestern Wyoming. The annual clovers are all found at comparatively low altitudes.

THE VETCHES AND VETCHLINGS.

Two species of the true vetches occur in this region and both are of value for forage. American vetch (*Vicia americana*) is found in rich, moist meadows and open thickets, and is regarded as a valuable native forage plant. It produces long trailing or climbing vines quite thickly covered with leaves and affords a good yield of forage. Narrow-leafed vetch (*V. linearis*) is much smaller than the preceding, occurs in drier situations, and, like it, is distributed throughout the entire region. It affords less forage than American vetch, and is less palatable, but thrives on soil too dry for that species, and hence replaces it in many localities. It is a hardy, aggressive plant, and rapidly takes possession of idle, broken land, under some circumstances becoming a weed, although not a troublesome one.

The vetchlings are better represented in this region than the true vetches, some five or six kinds being found, of which at least three are of value for forage. They are not very palatable in the fresh state, and hence are of more importance as hay plants. The most valuable sorts are the prairie vetchlings (*Lathyrus ornatus* and *L. polymorphus*) and marsh vetchling (*L. palustris*). The former are found chiefly in the central and southern portions of the region, while the latter occurs throughout.

Small prairie vetchling (*L. ornatus*) is usually found in dry prairies, and in some parts of the region, as in southeastern Wyoming, is very abundant. It fruits plentifully, and the seeds are said to be edible, comparing favorably with the common garden pea. The larger prairie vetchling (*L. polymorphus*) occurs in rather moister situations than the preceding and is a somewhat more robust plant with much larger flowers. It is very abundant in portions of central and southern Colorado, where it is regarded as a valuable element in native meadows.

Marsh vetchling is a much taller plant than either of the foregoing and occurs chiefly in rich, moist meadows and about the edges of thickets. It is frequently sufficiently abundant to form an important part of the hay, adding very materially to its feeding value. In some localities it is called "meadow pea."

Among other vetchlings occurring in this region of more or less value as forage plants are veiny-leafed vetchling (*Lathyrus venosus*), growing usually on sparsely wooded hillsides and river banks, and cream-colored vetchling (*L. ochroleucus*), found in similar situations to the preceding.

One of the most valuable leguminous plants found on the prairies is Dakota vetch (*Lotus americanus*) (see fig. 25), a bushy annual growing throughout the entire Rocky Mountain region. It is most abundant on sandy river bottoms, but also occurs on the drier uplands. Stock is very fond of it, either as pasturage or as hay. In the Upper Missouri region it is one of the most highly prized

FIG. 25.—Dakota vetch (*Lotus americanus*).

native forage plants, and the rancher who has a good lot of it in his meadows and pastures considers himself fortunate. As it is an annual it must be allowed to mature its seed and should not be grazed too closely nor cut too early. The blooming season is quite long, so that buds, flowers, and both green and mature fruits may often be seen on the plant at the same time. As a rule many of the seeds are ripened before haying time arrives, and it is a common practice among ranchers to use hay racks with tight bottoms in order to save the shattered seed that it may be scattered over thin places in the meadows.

THE LUPINES.

Although the wild lupines are so abundantly represented in this region, as to both kinds and individuals, they can hardly be regarded as of much value for forage from the fact that they are generally so unpalatable that stock will seldom eat them unless forced to do so by hunger. Sheep eat them more readily than other stock. Many of the species thrive on dry, rocky soils too poor to produce much other vegetation, and they probably do a great deal toward improving the fertility of these soils, and are thus indirectly beneficial; but many ranchers regard them as weeds, owing to their tendency to spread rapidly in overstocked pasture lands.

THE MILK-VETCHES.

The milk-vetches, or rattle-weeds, as some of them are called, are by far the best represented group of leguminous plants in the range region. Of the numerous sorts some are valuable forage plants, others are too small to be of any value or are so unpalatable that stock will not eat them, and a few—the so-called "loco weeds"—are injurious to stock under certain circumstances, causing considerable loss by killing the animals eating them.

The milk-vetches occur on a great variety of soil, from rich, moist bottom lands to dry, sterile, rocky, and gravelly ridges, often forming a large proportion of the vegetation. In some of the species the fruits are large and fleshy and are much sought after by stock, particularly by sheep. There are probably a great many kinds that are of more or less value as forage plants, but our knowledge of the real value of most of the species is very limited and reports are contradictory, some stockmen regarding certain sorts as injurious, while others

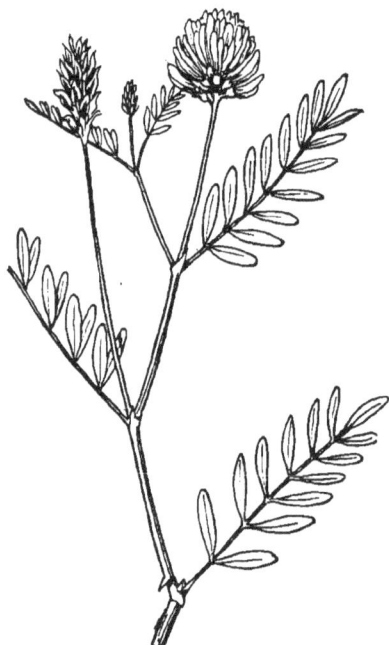

FIG. 26.—Prairie milk-vetch (*Astragalus adsurgens*).

maintain that they are valuable forage plants, stock eating them with the best of results.

Among the most common and valuable kinds are bristly-fruited milk-vetch (*Astragalus hypoglottis*), ground plum or buffalo pea (*A. crassicarpus*), larger ground plum (*A. mexicanus*), and prairie milk-vetch (*A. adsurgens*), (see fig. 26.) Other species, regarded by many as valuable, are Morton's milk-vetch (*A. mortoni*), zigzag milk-vetch (*A. flexuosus*), and slender milk-vetch (*A. gracilis*). Low milk-vetch (*A. lotiflorus*) and bitter milk-vetch (*A. bisulcatus*) are by some regarded as good forage plants and by others as injurious species. Some years ago the writer observed both cattle and horses eating considerable quantities of the former without any apparent ill effect, but the latter is so bitter and strong-scented that it would hardly seem possible that stock would eat much of it.

RUSHES AND SEDGES.

These grass-like plants play no small part in the forage supply and are of much more importance than is generally understood. There are almost as many kinds of rushes and sedges native to this region as there are grasses, and all are eaten by stock to a greater or less extent. Comparatively few kinds grow on the dry prairies and hills, most of them occurring in low prairies, meadows, and bogs. Sometimes the greater part of the hay obtained from wet, boggy meadows is made up of these plants. They are particularly abundant in some of the mountain meadows, frequently, especially early in the season, occupying the land almost to the exclusion of the grasses.

RUSHES.

There are at least six of the bulrushes that deserve mention as forage plants. These are meadow bulrush (*Scirpus atrovirens*), salt-marsh bulrush (*S. robustus*), river bulrush (*S. fluviatilis*), small-fruited bulrush (*S. microcarpus*), prairie bulrush (*S. campestris*), and alkali or chair-makers' bulrush (*S. americanus*). The best of these, though not necessarily the most abundant, are river bulrush, meadow bulrush, and salt-marsh bulrush. Alkali or chair-makers' bulrush (the former name is most used in this region) is one of the most abundant species, and, as its common name indicates, occurs on alkali flats along streams and elsewhere in moist soil containing large quantities of alkali. It is tough and wiry, but is often eaten by stock when better forage is scant.

Of the spike-rushes, common spike-rush (*Eleocharis palustris*) and flat-stemmed spike-rush (*E. acuminata*) are the most important. In wet meadows, particularly those that are overirrigated, these rushes are very abundant, sometimes forming the larger part of the vegetation. Some of the larger forms of common spike-rush yield a large amount of hay, but the quality is much inferior to that obtained from the grasses.

There are a dozen or more of the bog rushes found in the eastern Rocky Mountain region. All are tough and wiry and afford an inferior quality of forage, but a number of them are sufficiently abundant to form a large part of the vegetation in some of the native meadows. The species most frequently found are slender bog rush (*Juncus tenuis*), Torrey's bog rush (*J. torreyi*), Baltic bog rush (*J. balticus*), knotted bog rush (*J. nodosus*), Nevada bog rush (*J. nevadensis*), and mountain bog rush (*J. xiphioides montanus*).

The list of sedges is a long one, more than a hundred different kinds being found in the Rocky Mountain region. They furnish a better quality of forage, as a rule, than that obtained from the rushes. Some of the species grow on dry prairies and hillsides, but the majority prefer the moister soils of the valleys and lowlands. Sedges form a conspicuous part of the vegetation of the meadows and moist mountain sides at the higher altitudes. Some of the species are small and are of value only as pasturage, but many others are of sufficient size to yield a large amount of hay which compares favorably in quality with that obtained from grasses growing in similar situations.

On the dry uplands, thread-leafed sedge (*Carex filifolia*), often also called "wire-grass," and dwarf sedge (*C. stenophylla*) furnish pasturage, the former being very abundant on dry ridges in some localities and highly prized by stockmen. Dwarf sedge is often plentiful in dry meadows, where it is larger than on the uplands. In swales and dry meadows silvery-top sedge (*C. siccata*), clustered field-sedge (*C. marcida*), and Douglas sedge (*C. douglasii*) are of considerable value for both hay and pasturage. There are a great many different forms of the Douglas sedge, some of them large and affording a good yield of hay, and others too small for anything but pasturage. The species is one of the most abundant in the sections nearer the mountains and also ascends to the higher altitudes. Brown-top sedge (*C. festiva*) is also abundant and valuable, but usually occurs in moister situations than the last. In wet, boggy meadows the sedges sometimes compose more of the vegetation than do the grasses. This is particularly the case at the higher altitudes or above 7,000 or 8,000 feet. The species most commonly found in these meadows are tussock sedge (*C. stricta*), bottle sedge (*C. utriculata*, and var. *minor*), Nebraska sedge (*C. nebraskensis*), woolly-fruited sedge (*C. lanuginosa*), and giant sedge (*C. aristata*). All produce a relatively large amount of leafage, and when cut in proper season afford hay of average quality.

MISCELLANEOUS NATIVE FORAGE PLANTS.

There are many miscellaneous plants native to this region that help to make up the general forage supply. These are mostly plants that the uninformed individual would regard as weeds, but which, under the conditions prevailing on the range, form an important part of the annual supply of stock feed. On the plains and foothills this vegetation consists very largely of the various kinds of "sage" and saltworts, plants characteristic of the arid and semiarid West. In the mountains it consists mainly of shrubby willows, mountain mahogany, shrubby cinquefoil, and purshia. There is a great variety of plants called "sage" on the range, as, for example, the bitter sages, or "sage-brush" (*Artemisia* spp.); green sages, or "rabbit-brush" (*Bigelovia* spp.); salt-sage (*Atriplex* spp.); sweet sage, or winterfat (*Eurotia lanata*), etc.

THE BITTER SAGES.

The bitter sages, or sage-brushes, are most of them so bitter that stock will not eat them as a general thing, except in times of scarcity of forage. Sheep eat the sage-brush more often than do any other of the domestic animals. They do not make a general diet of it, but eat small quantities now and then, as if for a tonic or appetizer. Bud brush or spring sage (*Artemisia spinescens*) is probably the most valuable of this group of sages. It is most abundant in the Red Desert of Wyoming, and extends into the arid regions to the southwest. The masses of young leaves and flowers are much relished by sheep, and the plant is regarded as an important member of the forage-producing species of the desert. Silvery sage (*A. cana*) is probably the next most valuable of the bitter sages. When browsed closely it produces a great many annual shoots, which are quite succulent and are eaten by sheep to a considerable extent.

THE SALT-SAGES.

The salt-sages are of much more importance as forage plants than the bitter sages. There are more than a dozen species native to this region, and all are of value for forage. In some sections, as in central Wyoming and in the Red Desert, these salt-sages, or "salt-bushes," furnish more of the forage than all the other plants combined. The kinds of most importance in this region are Nuttall's salt-sage (*Atriplex nuttallii*), spiny salt-sage (*A. confertifolia*), hoary salt-sage, or

FIG. 27.—Shad scale (*Atriplex canescens*).

shad scale (*A. canescens*) (see fig. 27), Nelson's salt-sage (*A. pabularis*), silvery salt-sage (*A. argentea*), tumbling salt-sage (*A. volutans*), and spreading salt-sage (*A. expansa*). All are annuals except the first three, which are perennials and are of especial importance for winter pasturage. The leaves, fruits, and young shoots are relished by all kinds of stock. Of the three, Nuttall's salt-sage is probably the most valuable.

The salt-sages thrive on land strongly impregnated with alkali, and so dry that but little other vegetation will exist upon it, and as there are many thousands of acres of such land in this region these plants are of particular importance. In certain districts, as along the Green River in Wyoming and also in the central part of the State, there are extensive areas in which the water supply is so limited that stock can not be kept on them during the summer. Here it is that the salt-sages thrive, and are of especial value for winter forage. During the growing season the plants make a good development, as they are not kept back by grazing, and the ripened fruits and " sun-cured" leaves, together with the young shoots, make excellent forage for winter, when, since the snow furnishes the animals with water, the stock can be brought to these regions. Thus it is that these desert areas become valuable winter pastures and furnish food for many thousands of sheep, cattle, and horses for about four months of the year. Stockmen, especially those owning large droves of sheep, are almost as anxious to establish and maintain their rights to " winter ranges" on these desert areas as they are to secure their "share" of the summer range on the prairies and in the mountains.

Under this system of winter grazing the condition of these salt-sage pasture lands is continually improving. This is probably due to the enriching of the land from the droppings of the animals, and to the increased production of new shoots by the perennial sages, resulting from the close browsing by the animals during winter, followed by an undisturbed period of growth in the summer.

The annual salt-sages are valuable principally for summer and autumn forage, not usually being persistent enough to be of much importance for winter use. However, under certain circumstances, the fallen leaves and fruits may be collected by the wind into little piles in depressions of the ground, or behind shrubs and other persistent plants, and are picked up by sheep or other stock. Under ordinary conditions all of the salt-sages mentioned in the above list produce an abundance of seed, and in most cases it is easily gathered. In view of the recognized value of these plants for forage it would seem well worth while to attempt to grow the better sorts under cultivation. There are many localities where they could be used to advantage.

WINTERFAT.

One of the most highly prized of the sages is winterfat or sweet sage (*Eurotia lanata*). (See fig. 28.) It is a rather small, woolly, half-shrubby perennial, found throughout the Rocky Mountain region in the dry soil of the plains and foothills. It is of most importance for winter pasturage and is esteemed not only for its feeding value, but also for a beneficial effect which it is supposed to have on the health of stock eating it. It usually fruits abundantly, and the great fattening qualities attributed to it are no doubt largely due to the fact that the matured fruits compose a large part of the forage obtained by the animals.

Winterfat grows readily from the seed and could undoubtedly be cultivated to good advantage in many localities.

GREASEWOOD.

Another plant of great value for forage on dry, sterile, strongly alkaline soil is greasewood (*Sarcobatus vermiculatus*). (See figs. 3 and 29.) It is more or less abundant throughout the entire region and is of especial importance in the bad lands and in sterile, broken areas on bluffs along the streams, and on the so-called "black alkali" spots in the valleys and plains. It is a scraggy, thorny shrub from 2 to 10 feet high, with fleshy, succulent leaves, and usually produces an abundance of fruit.' The leaves, fruit, and young shoots are eaten by stock to such an

Fig. 28.—Winterfat (*Eurotia lanata*).   Fig. 29.—Greasewood (*Sarcobatus vermiculatus*).

extent that in some localities the plants are kept so closely browsed as to be ultimately destroyed. Under ordinary conditions this plant furnishes a large amount of forage and is particularly valuable, since it will thrive on soil that will not even produce sage-brush. As stated elsewhere in this report, "sage-brush" land is easily subdued, and under irrigation produces excellent crops of grain, alfalfa, etc., while "greasewood" land is regarded as of but little agricultural value by ranchers because of the quantity and character of the alkali contained in it.

MISCELLANEOUS.

Among other plants of weedy habit which add considerably to the forage supply in some localities are the goosefoots or lambs-quarters

(*Chenopodium* spp.) and the knotweeds (*Polygonum* spp.). There are a half-dozen species of each that occur in sufficient abundance to be of value. They are usually found in broken soil along banks and trails and about desiccated ponds, occupying land in which grasses will not thrive or from which they have been killed out.

In the higher foothills and mountains the browsing is principally furnished by such shrubby plants as the willows, shrubby cinque-foil (*Potentilla fruticosa*), mountain mahogany (*Cercocarpus parvifolius*), Torrey's nine-bark (*Physocarpus torreyi*), and Purshia (*Purshia tridentata*). These are all often so extensively eaten by stock that it is difficult to find a plant showing anything like its natural habit of growth. This is particularly true on the sheep ranges. Shrubby cinque-foil was seen in great abundance the past season (1897) on the Big Horn Mountains, but wherever the sheep had been ranged to any considerable extent the bushes were so closely browsed that it was difficult to get good botanical specimens. The same was true to a great extent with the several species of shrubby willows occurring on the same mountains.

Wild liquorice (*Glycyrrhiza lepidota*) is abundant in low, sandy prairies and river bottoms throughout the range region. This plant, regarded as a troublesome weed in the eastern prairie States, is highly esteemed as a forage plant by many ranchers. It is often present in abundance in the hay obtained from river-bottom meadows,

FIG. 30.—Montana bush-pea (*Thermopsis montana*).

and such hay is regarded as having high feeding value. In the Big Horn Basin it is frequently called "wild alfalfa," and many tons of it are cut annually.

In addition to the various plants mentioned in the preceding pages, all of recognized value as forage producers, there is a long list of plants which, although each is perhaps of but little value in itself, when they are considered in the aggregate the amount of forage afforded by them is large. Such are the prairie clovers (*Petalostemon* spp. and *Psoralea* spp.), the Daleas (*Dalea alopecuroides* and *D. aurea*), the bush-peas (*Thermopsis montana* (see fig. 30) and *T. rhomboidea*), the herbaceous cinque-foils (*Potentilla* spp.), wild asters, and many others.

IMPROVEMENT OF THE RANGES.

One of the most important factors in the improvement of the range conditions would be the establishment of some system of control which would allow each rancher the exclusive right to graze his stock on a given piece of land for a long term of years. As long as the "open range" is "free to all," ranchmen will continue to try to get their "share" of it and there will be no possibility of any substantial improvement. Under the present conditions there is no incentive for the rancher to make any special efforts to improve the range except in so far as it has to do with the immediate necessities of his stock. He knows that if his stock does not eat the grass, that of somebody else will, and naturally he thinks he might as well benefit by it as anyone. In his efforts to get his "share" he contributes to the general destruction instead of trying to avert it.

It is argued that if the rancher could secure a long lease to a portion of these public lands it would then be to his interest to improve and maintain their productivity. He could then afford to build fences and adopt other measures for the betterment of his holdings, being sure that he and not someone else would get the benefit of his endeavors.

With the recent rapid increase in the number of tilled ranches and the growing tendency toward the raising of more coarse forage for winter feeding, it ought to be possible to handle more stock than formerly instead of less, as is the case at the present time. Thus in the Big Horn Basin and elsewhere in northern Wyoming ranchers assert that they can easily raise winter feed for more stock than their summer range will carry in its present depleted condition. This statement is borne out by the fact that on many ranches one may see large quantities of surplus hay, often representing portions of crops of two or three years. There are other districts in which the practice of growing forage for winter use should be greatly extended. The range could supply plenty of pasturage for a part of the year, but is insufficient for both summer and winter forage. Millet, rye, oats, field peas, rape, sorghum, and other forage crops can some of them be grown with at least a fair degree of success in most localities in this region, and an extension of their cultivation would have a beneficial effect on the open range, in that it would be less closely grazed.

An important problem to be considered in connection with the improvement of range conditions is that of the water supply, particularly as to the conservation and more equable distribution of the annual rainfall. Something can be done by the individual efforts of the stockmen, but if much permanent good is to be accomplished the united efforts of the community and possibly the aid of the local or the General Government will need to be turned in this direction.

The conservation of water in this manner would serve a twofold purpose. Not only would it render possible the irrigation of more land adapted to the growing of forage and other crops and the better irrigation of land already under cultivation, but water would also be provided for stock in places convenient to the grazing lands, and much of the injury to the range due to excessive trampling would be avoided. As the laws governing the distribution of water for irrigation become better understood and more justly applied much of the present unequal distribution of the water from the running streams will be corrected, and stock will be better supplied with drinking water and more forage will be produced. Under the present conditions one may frequently see a man injuring his meadows and fields by using too much water, while those of his neighbor some miles down the valley are suffering, perhaps totally ruined, for lack of water.

In a region varying so widely in soil and climatic conditions it is not to be expected that any one or two grasses or forage plants can be introduced to meet all the requirements. Timothy, redtop, alfalfa, and other of the commoner "tame" sorts have shown themselves admirably adapted for certain localities. Smooth brome is being used with fine success in some of the drier sections. But other varieties are needed, and the only way to select them is through careful experimentation. It is not necessary that these experiments should be elaborate. Each rancher should test one or two of the hardy grasses or forage plants in a small way each season, and thus determine for himself what kinds are best adapted to his needs and to the conditions prevailing in his locality.

These experiments should not be confined to "tame" or introduced sorts, but should be extended to desirable native kinds, such as have been mentioned in the preceding pages. There is no locality without native grasses or forage plants that are worthy of trial under cultivation, and anyone can, with but little trouble, obtain enough seed for such a test. Some farmers are already following this plan, and while some attempts meet with failure, others give very encouraging results—so much so that the great value of some of the native species is clearly demonstrated for certain localities, and in some cases the seed is being placed on the market, as for example, slender wheat-grass (*Agropyron tenerum*) and reed canary-grass (*Phalaris arundinacea*). It is extremely likely that there are native varieties of grasses and clovers which will be found to be well adapted for cultivation above the altitudinal limits of timothy, alfalfa, and other of the commonly cultivated grass and forage crops. Among such may be mentioned Nevada blue grass (*Poa nevadensis*), Wyoming blue grass (*P. wheeleri*), rough-leafed bent (*Agrostis asperifolia*), mountain foxtail (*Alopecurus occidentalis*), short-awned brome (*Bromus breviaristatus*), western brome (*B. pumpellianus*), Beckwith's clover (*Trifolium beckwithii*), and long-stalked clover (*T. longipes*).

As a general rule ranchmen assert that the only treatment required for the restoration of the range is rest, but this under the present conditions is practically an impossibility. Moreover, in some localities the work of destruction has gone so far that something more than mere rest is necessary. The valuable grasses have been killed out and their places taken by plants of weedy habit, of little, if any, value for forage, or the land is without vegetation at all. To reclaim such areas arti- ficial seeding is necessary. With these places again seeded and pro- ducing forage it will be easier to give at least a partial rest to the lands on which there still remains enough of the good grasses to accom- plish natural reseeding. Many farmers and ranchmen in the North- west have been able to materially increase the stock-carrying capacity of their pasture lands by scattering over the worn spots the seed of such grasses as western wheat-grass (*Agropyron spicatum*), prairie June- grass (*Koeleria cristata*), Kentucky blue grass, and smooth brome. Sometimes these areas are harrowed or "disked" after seeding, and sometimes not. One practice is to seed while the ground is wet and drive stock over the land to work the seed into the soil.

When wheat-grass is already present in considerable quantity the pro- ductiveness may be vastly improved by "disking" up the land. Some farmers even go so far as to plow up the land and then allow the wheat- grass to come in again, which it does in a very short time. This latter method keeps the land in better condition and gets rid of weeds, and is a good practice to follow on the smaller ranches. When seed can be had it would be a good plan to sow a small quantity of prairie June- grass, bench-land spear-grass, smooth brome, or other of the better native or introduced sorts, that the land may be occupied at once. Sometimes such annuals as millet, oats, rye, and sorghum can be used to advantage. The practice of fencing the range in such a manner that one portion of it may be grazed while the other is resting is to be recommended. This allows the grasses opportunity to recuperate and to produce seed occasionally.

If each ranchman and farmer could but keep the land under his own immediate control up to the point of greatest productivity the indirect effect upon the open range through decreased demands upon it would be decidedly beneficial. In the absence of some rational system of control for the open range little can be done in a direct way to bring about better forage conditions upon it, but much can and will be done on private holdings as soon as the ranchers realize, as they are begin- ning to do, that they can not be continually taking from their meadow and pasture lands without adding something to them by care, occasional reseeding, and cultivation.

INDEX TO BOTANICAL NAMES.

77

www.ingramcontent.com/pod-product-compliance
Lightning Source LLC
Chambersburg PA
CBHW021522270326
41930CB00008B/1050